CW00983174

A selection o
Best Inns &
in the Midlands

Compiled by:	Douglas Aitchison
	Pauline Hayward
	Richard MacPherson
	Robin Morris
Edited by:	James Lawrence

CONTENTS

Published by
Bracken Publishing
Bracken House, 199a Holt Road
Cromer, Norfolk NR27 9JN

ISBN 1 871614 12 0

Printed by Broadgate Printers, Aylsham, Norfolk.

May 1992

Others in this series

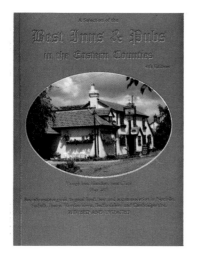

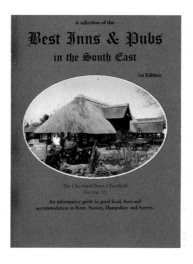

Also published: Best Hotels & Restaurants in the Eastern Counties.

Available in most bookshops and some pubs within area, or by writing to Bracken Publishing, enclosing payment of £3.50 each (£4.00 for Best Inns & Pubs in Eastern Counties), to include postage.

Important

Please note:-

1. *Dishes quoted from menus are examples only, and not necessarily available at all times.*

2. *The listing of brewers' beers and lagers does not mean that their full range is necessarily available.*

3. *Prices, where quoted, may alter during the currency of this guide.*

4. *Every effort is made to ensure accuracy, but inevitably circumstances' change and errors and omissions may occur. Therefore the publisher cannot accept liability for any consequences arising therefrom.*

5. *This is a selection: it is not claimed that all the best inns and pubs are featured.*

6. *Your comments about any establishment, favourable or not, are particularly welcome. Correspondents who especially impress the editor will receive a complimentary copy of the next edition.*

7. *Special note to publicans: if your house is not included, please do not be offended! The area covered is very large, and time limited. If you serve good food in pleasant surrounds, please write and we will visit you.*

FURTHER COPIES OF THIS OR OUR OTHER GUIDES
MAY BE OBTAINED BY WRITING TO:-

Bracken Publishing
Bracken House
199a Holt Road
Cromer
Norfolk NR27 9JN

Eastern Counties Inns & Pubs
Eastern Counties Hotels & Restaurants
Cotswolds, Thames Valley & Chilterns Inns & Pubs
West Country Inns & Pubs
South East Inns & Pubs

Enclose payment of £3.50 per book (£4.00 for Eastern Counties Inns & Pubs), to include postage etc. No orders will be accepted without prior payment, other than from recognised book retailers.

PUBLIC BARS

The bars in our friendly locals are a cherished forum for debate and free exchange of views.

But there are many countries in the world where merely expressing an opinion can put you behind bars of a quite different kind; where torture and murder of innocents are routine.

For 30 years, Amnesty International has campaigned successfully to help these brave people. Please spare a thought, and a little cash – even if only the price of a pint – while you enjoy our great English pubs in complete freedom.

Please send donations to:–

Amnesty International,
c/o Bracken Publishing,
Bracken House,
199a Holt Road, Cromer,
Norfolk NR27 9JN

THANK YOU

AMNESTY
INTERNATIONAL

THE PACK HORSE INN

Little Longstone, Bakewell.   Tel. (062 987) 471

                Location: Centre of hamlet.
            Credit cards: Not accepted.
                 Bitters: Marstons Pedigree, Burtons.
                 Lagers: Heineken.

Examples of bar meals (lunch & evening, 7 days): *steak & kidney pie, aromatic spicy chicken, tipsy braised steak (in barley wine & whisky), curries, Cumberland sausage, vegetarian dishes. Speciality nights eg 'Orient Express', French, Best of British.*

The Peak District is widely considered the most scenic part of this region. Apart from the stern beauty of the landscape, there are delightful little hamlets tucked in amongst the hills. This one has the considerable benefit of a gem of a 16th century cottage pub, featured in major guides, and Camra's 'Pub of the month'. The two bars are very pretty, without being twee, having open fires, beam and plank ceiling, rock asphalt floors and limestone churt walls. Add to this an adornment of fresh flowers, and the effect is most pleasing to the eye. Other parts of the anatomy are also well catered for: all the food is homemade, and the portions generous. Local regulars are always to be found here, indeed proprietors (for six years) Lynne and Mark Lythgoe are locals themselves, but the many visitors are made welcome, and children, too, if well behaved. Rabbits, goats and lambs in the garden should hold their attention!

YE OLDE NAGS HEAD HOTEL

Castleton.   Tel. (0433) 620248

Location:	Village centre.
Credit cards:	Access, Visa, Diners, Amex, Switch.
Accommodation:	6 doubles, 2 twins, all en suite, tv's, direct phones, trouser presses. 4-poster beds. 1 whirlpool bath. From £41 single, £52 dble. 2/3 day breaks.
Bitters:	Stones, Bass.
Lagers:	Carling, Tennents LA.

Examples of bar meals (lunch & evening, 7 days): *homemade steak & kidney pie, steaks, lasagne, filled Yorkshire pudding, spare ribs in barbecue sauce, crab creole, plaice stuffed with prawns on lobster sauce, salads, sandwiches, daily specials.*
Examples of restaurant meals (as above): *smoked salmon & prawn crouton, asparagus & ham pancake, chicken & scampi in lobster sauce, venison in red wine sauce, veal mozzarella, steak Roquefort, halibut Clarinda, turbot champagne. Trad. Sun. roasts.*

Castleton's narrow streets and stone cottages cluster along the banks of a clear, burbling river in the shadow of the grey ruins of Peveril Castle. It's an area renowned as much for its beauty below ground as above; a few minutes walk takes you to the Peak Cavern, and also very near are the Speedwell Cavern, the Treak and the famous Blue John Mine. With so much to see, an overnight stay is recommended at this special 300-year-old coaching inn. Its truly old world character – log fires, antique furniture, fresh flowers, individual bedrooms – makes it worth the visit on its own merit. Being close to major conurbations it's also ideal for business people. Mrs Walker is the long standing landlady, and she welcomes children. Car park.

THREE STAGS HEADS

Wardlow Mires, Tideswell.   Tel. (0298) 872268
Location: On A623 at junction with B6049.
Credit cards: Not accepted.
Bitters: Theakstons, Youngers.
Lagers: None on draught, but good bottled selection.

Examples of bar meals (12 – 10pm, every day except Monday. Opens 7pm Monday. Open normally on Bank Hols): *duck in ginger, cous-cous, pork casserole, vegetable biriani, vegetable bake, ancient recipes eg roast shoulder of lamb with wine sauce. Cheesecake, chocolate fudge cake.*

'Olde Worlde' is a phrase which has come to represent gaudy pastiche and plastic imitation, but here is the authentic article. It's simple and unique, without phoney memorabilia, and especially no jukeboxes etc. Two separate bars and a little dining room have flagstoned floors and open fire – basic, but cosy and friendly. It were not always so; footpad Anthony Lingard earned the distinction of being the last man in England to be publically gibbeted, right opposite the pub, in 1816. The history dates back probably to the 14th century, but for more details ask Geoff and Pat Fuller, who've been here just three years or so. They are making quite a name for excellent and unusual food (rated by major guides), served on plates made in the pottery workshop in the adjacent barn. This is marvellous hiking and potholing country, but the pub draws custom from miles around, especially as it is open 11am to 11pm most days. Children accepted if well-behaved. Car park opposite.

THE MINERS STANDARD

West Bank, Winster, nr Matlock.   Tel. (0629 88) 279
           Location: On B5056.
     Credit cards: Not accepted.
            Bitters: Marstons Pedigree, Theakstons XB, Old Baily, Timothy Taylors.
             Lagers: Carling, Fosters, Stella Artois, Dansk LA.

Examples from lunch menu (7 days): *leek & stilton soup, steak & kidney pie, chicken tikka, curry, chilli, steaks, plaice, Barnsley chop, spicy sausages, fried liver & onions, vegetarian dish of day, ploughman's. Trad. Sun. roast.*
Examples from evening menu (7 days): *veal in cream & herb sauce, pork in green pepper sauce, scampi, steak Diane, gammon & pineapple, vegetarian dish, chef's specials.*
NB restaurant open Thurs. – Sun. evening, and Sun. lunch.

The last remaining Tudor pub in an historic village derives its name from the Henry VIII standard measure used in lead mining. Carefully restored, it retains the original oak beams and brickwork, open fires, and a number of especially interesting features: a collection of British minerals is one, and the solid oak bar with stone slab facing. Also, look for a glass-topped pit in front of the fire, with a mysterious face in it. A friendly spirit reputedly haunts the place – a former miner, perhaps, who still enjoys the panoramic view from the function room, across lovely countryside to White Peak. Jane Saville and family have been here over four years and welcome well behaved children, who have a special room and a playground in the garden. Barbecues are frequently held on the patio at weekends. Skittles, darts and dominoes. Live entertainment twice a month. Two large car parks. Featured in Camra guide.

THE VAULTS & SCOFF'S BAR & RESTAURANT

Coldwell Street, Wirksworth.   Tel. (0629) 822186

Location:	Town centre.
Credit cards:	Access, Visa, Diners, Amex.
Accommodation:	4 dbles, en suite, with tv's, tea & coffee. £36 pp dble, £42 sgle.
Bitters:	Bass, Mansfield, Theakstons, guests.
Lagers:	Red Stripe, Carling, Tennents Extra, Fosters.

Examples of bar meals (lunch & evening, 7 days): *cottage pie, steak & kidney pie, curry, beef in Old Peculier, vegetarian fruit curry, Hungarian fish casserole, moussaka, blackboard specials. Orlando lemon cheesecake, chocolate fudge cake.*
Examples of restaurant meals (as above): *smoked fish mousse, prawn bisque; Scoff's special (fillet of pork in orange sauce), steaks, roast duck with gooseberry & beer sauce, chef's special chicken (in white wine & mushroom), paella, poached brill cardinal, scampi thermidor, regular specials. Dutch apple pie, charlotte royal. Trad. Sun. roasts.*

Great changes have taken place here in the two years since Mick and Lesley Andrews took over. It was just a town centre alehouse, but total (and expensive) refurbishment has created a bright, spacious air, excellent accommodation, and a function room for 20 – 25. The new dining room is most attractive, separated from the two bars by arches, and all thickly carpeted. Equally radical have been improvements to the range and quality of food. As the examples above indicate, the menus are varied and stylish. The building is 300 years old, and was a whisky blending house – old prints of whisky and brandy advertisements decorate the walls. Wirksworth is a pleasant, historic market town, on the edge of The Peaks, yet not too far from industrial centres, so this is a most suitable spot to stay whether on business or pleasure. Children welcome. Adjacent free car park.

THE DRUID INN

Main Street, Birchover, nr Matlock.

Tel. (0629) 650302
Fax. (0629) 650559

Location: Edge of village, 2 miles from A6, ¹/₂ mile from B5056.
Credit cards: Access, Visa, Mastercard, Amex, Switch.
Bitters: Marstons, Ruddles, Webster's Yorkshire.
Lagers: Fosters, Heineken.

Examples of bar meals (lunch & evening 7 days. Closed Christmas Day and Boxing Day evening): *Szechuan spare ribs, chicken fahjitas, Bombay potatoes, bacon steak with gooseberry sauce, Peakland beef casserole, meat & potato pie, steak & mussel pie, Roman lamb stew, loin of lamb stuffed with apricots & thyme & topped with plum sauce, Rowtor medieval chicken, steaks, cod & broccoli topped with cheese & white wine sauce, trout topped with prawns & mussels, fruit & vegetable lasagne/curry, savoury bake, ros codia (Arabian rice dish).*

Right next to this 18th century pub stand the strange Rowtor Rocks, supposedly once inhabited by Druids. Perhaps they resent the intrusion: when landlord Brian Bunce arrived here 10 years ago, he was struck in the face by a falling stool on his first visit to the cellar! Undaunted, he and manager Nigel Telford have built this into one of the most succesful eating houses in the region, recommended by virtually all the main guides. The size of the menu is simply staggering, and it caters for every conceivable taste, even vegan. One may enjoy it in any of four rooms, including a garden room for non-smokers. Children welcome if eating. Darts. Terrace. Ample parking.

THE BOAT HOUSE

Dale Road, Matlock.   Tel. (0629) 583776

Location:	On A6, ¹/₄ mile from town centre.
Credit cards:	Access, Visa, Mastercard, Eurocard, Luncheon Vouchers.
Accommodation:	One single, one double, one twin, one family, from £13.50 pp
Bitters:	Kimberley.
Lagers:	Stella Artois, Heineken.

Examples of bar meals (lunch & evening, 7 days. Not Sunday evenings in winter): *lample pie (with lamb & apples), salmon bake, Caribbean chicken, beef in beer, pork in cider, 'zoomamadooma' (vegetarian), scampi, trout, burgers, salads. Children's menu. Trad. Sun roast £4.95, children £3.95.*

At the gateway to the glorious Peak District, 'Boathouse' seems an unlikely name for a pub, until you know that a ferryboat used to operate across the river Derwent, which flows virtually past the door. Being on the A6, there's always a good mix of passers by and regulars, and the atmosphere is friendly, the service relaxed but efficient. The two bars are fully carpeted, have bench seating, a real stonework fire and all the character one might expect of a 200-year-old building. Dogs and children are welcome, and there is a family room, plus tables and chairs outside. Bedrooms are comfortable, and the location alone makes this a desirable place to stay, being so close to The Peaks, Chatsworth, Heights of Abraham etc, as well as being just yards from the town centre, yet room rates are very reasonable. Pool table. Parking for 30.

11

THE RAGLEY

Deepdale Lane, Barrow-on-Trent.   Tel. (0332) 703919

Location: Off A5132, one mile from village centre.
Credit cards: Access, Visa.
Bitters: Marstons Pedigree, Bass, Bass Special, Worthington. Guinness.
Lagers: Carling, Tennents Pilsner, Tennents Extra, Tennents LA.

Examples of bar meals (lunchtime 7 days, evenings Wed – Sat): *lasagne, cottage pie, pizza, chicken Kiev, steaks, goujons of salmon, scampi, plaice, burgers, chilli, curry, omelettes, nut cutlets, veg. pancake rolls, salads, ploughman's. Occasional specials. Children's menu.*
Examples of restaurant meals (Fri & Sat evenings, plus Sun roast lunch): *turkey escalope with redcurrant & cranberry sauce, roast guinea fowl with cream & green pepper sauce, fillet of pork with black butter, hunters casserole, stuffed trout with parsley butter, darne of salmon with orange sauce.*

On the southern fringes of outer Derby, yet in a rural setting of four acres bordering on the Trent-Mersey Canal, this is a stylish reproduction of a large Tudor pub, though parts of it are 200 years old. Both bar and restaurant are heavily timbered and have brickwork double fireplace, and leaded windows in keeping with the period. However, there are concessions to the advantages of modernity, including central heating, and dart board and pool table. An upstairs function room has its own bar, and can take up to 120 – a super spot for a wedding reception, having parking for 150 cars, and huge lawns to the water's edge. The beer garden has an aviary and play area, and there's also a children's room inside. Paul and Geoffrey Harman (father and son) have run this family concern for two years – Paul is a trained chef. Good facilities for disabled. Moorings. Calke Abbey nearby.

THE CHESTERFIELD ARMS

Hartshorne, Burton-on-Trent.   Tel. (0283) 217267
Location: Edge of village, 1¹/₂ miles off A50.
Credit cards: Not accepted.
Bitters: Bass (range).
Lagers: Carling, Tennents, Tennents LA.

Examples of bar meals (lunchtime only, Mon. – Sat.): *homemade steak pie, Chesterfield grill, plaice, haddock, scampi, seafood platter, roast chicken, omelettes, salads, ploughman's, burgers, cobs, sandwiches, homemade soups in winter, occasional specials eg lasagne. Filled rolls Sunday lunch.*

Although food is served only at lunchtime, the friendly atmosphere is always there, served by Alan and Pat, who've been here for around five years. They have plans to build up the facilities of their 18th century pub, named after Lord Chesterfield, who had large estates locally. At present they have a large lounge with timbered ceiling, carefully modernised and luxuriously appointed with upholstered seating. Then there's the tap room, with large brick open fireplace and log fire. Finally, the simple pool room doubles as a family room. Outside, the beer garden occupies no less than one quarter of an acre, complete with swings and more planned. Calke Abbey is only four miles away, and those with an intellectual interest in beer should visit the brewing museums in nearby Burton. This is good walking country, and here one is just over the border into Derbyshire. Parking for approx. 60 cars.

THE JUG & GLASS

Ashbourne Road, Hartington, nr Buxton.

Tel. (0298) 84224
Fax. (0298) 84787

Location: On A515, by Hartington turn-off.
Credit cards: Not accepted.
Bitters: Ruddles Best & County, Marston's Pedigree, Owd Rodger, Bass, Mansfield, Kimberley Classic, Tennents LA, guests.
Lagers: Red Stripe, Carling, Heineken.

Examples of bar meals (lunch & evening, 7 days): *homemade soups, steaks, gammon, scampi, haddock, vegetable lasagne/stroganoff, ploughman's, daily specials eg filled Yorkshire pudding, chilli, jumbo sausage with rich onion gravy. American apple & cream, double chocolate gateau, cheesecake.*
Examples of restaurant meals (every evening & Sun lunch): *self-carve roast joints (beef, lamb, pork), to order given 24 hrs notice (min 4 pers). £9.50 for 3 courses & coffee.*

One of the smallest pubs in Derbyshire has one of the biggest reputations for good value food, and one of the largest selections of cask beers. It is also the second highest in the county (the pub has its own snow plough!), commanding marvellous views over moorland. Dating from the 16th century, it was popular with workers on the High Peaks Railway, one of whom died here. It is not he, however, who is the 'presence': she is known as 'Martha'. Landlord (and ex-Para) John Bryan has served 12 years at The Jug and Glass, which for the last 11 has been featured in a major national good pub guide. The carvery is especially noted, but John charges a half pint 'Carver's Grog' if you ask him to carve! Children welcome – play area and occasional barbecues in garden. SPECIAL NOTE: annual beer festival September 4th, 5th & 6th, 1992.

THE LINCOLNSHIRE POACHER

161 – 163 Mansfield Road, Nottingham.   Tel. (0602) 411584

Location: ¹/₂ mile from city centre.
Credit cards: Not accepted.
Bitters: Batemans, Marston's Pedigree, guests.

Examples of bar meals (lunchtime every day, evenings Mon – Fri): *sausage & mash, chilli, prawn risotto with garlic bread, tagliatelle pesto, mushroom stroganoff, spicy bean & vegetable casserole, garlic mushrooms with crusty bread, ploughman's.*

Most towns are twinned with others on the continent, but it must be a very rare, if not unique arrangement between pubs. This former 18th century alehouse is linked with "In der Wildeman" in Amsterdam – if you would like to know more ask landlord Neil Kelso. If the food is as good over there then the Dutch can count themselves fortunate: it's all homecooked (no chips), and vegetarian dishes comprise about half the menu. Most of the major good pub guides rate it highly, as they do the beer (stored in very deep cellars). Neil is something of an expert on the subject, having been a brewing chemist. No clattering machines assault the eardrums; the wood-panelled lounge is a restful room, and there's also a conservatory with pine tables and wooden floors. Those who appreciate the unusual should cast an eye over the antique bottles and pump clip collection. Also uncommon is the facility to provide your own menu for a private dinner party! Children welcome inside at lumchtimes only, but there is a beer garden.

THE LORD NELSON INN

Lord Nelson Street, Sneinton.   Tel. (0602) 504801

        Location: Off Sneinton Dale, in the east of the city
    Credit cards: Not accepted.
          Bitters: Kimberley, Kimberley Classic.
          Lagers: Heineken, Stella Artois.

Examples of bar meals (lunchtime every day except Sundays): *homemade soup, smoked mackerel, roast English topside, homecooked ham, roast chicken, fresh salmon, salad Nicoise, hot dish of the day (winter)*.

"The only country pub situated in the city of Nottingham" – if that seems a contradiction, go and see for yourself. Built as a farmhouse 500 years ago and licensed for the last 200, that "olde worlde" quality unique to country pubs is to be found amongst the nooks and crannies, exposed timbers, nick-nacks and brass kettles – altogether very cosy. If you hadn't planned to eat, a glimpse of the cold table might change your mind. The tempting display of homecooked meats and fish is well known in the area, and very reasonably priced. In the evening food gives way to good beer and conversation, or live music on occasion. Gordon Good has been the landlord for about three years; he welcomes children and has a garden and terrace with seating. So, after a day in the bustle of the city, unwind and refresh yourself in this little outpost of the countryside. Greens Windmill nearby.

THE HORSE & GROOM

Moorgreen, Newthorpe.   Tel. (0773) 713417
    Location: Rural area, approx. 7 miles from Nottingham city centre.
Credit cards: Access, Visa, Switch.
    Bitters: Kimberley.
    Lagers: Stella Artois, Heineken.

Examples of bar meals (lunch & evening, 7 days): *lasagne verdi, rib eye steak, gammon with pineapple or egg, Cumberland sausage in long roll, plaice, cod, vegetable lasagne, daily specials.*
Examples of restaurant meals (as above): *steaks, roast, Barnsley chop, cajun chicken, chicken tikka masala, darne of wild salmon, scampi, mushroom quiche. Homemade fruit pie, light sponge pudding, cappuccino log. Trad. Sun. roasts (in bar also).*

Sunday, the day most of us like to get out and about, is yet the most awkward when it comes to finding refreshment. It is therefore worth making a special mental note of this popular pub, for it offers the rare blessing of all-day opening on Sundays. Of uncertain age, it is very much in keeping with tradition: two open fires make their inimitable contribution to a warm and friendly atmosphere, hops and dried flowers remind one of summer, and racing silks and saddles are colourful and interesting decor. Landlord since autumn 1991, Stephen Wisniewski has several years in the trade behind him and likes to socialize – quiz nights, silly darts, bar skittles and discos are some of the regular entertainments. Children are welcome, and the garden has a play area and barbecue. Near to D.H. Lawrence museum. Ample parking.

17

OLD PLOUGH

Main Street, Egmanton, nr Newark.   Tel. (0777) 870532
          Location: Village centre.
     Credit cards: Access, Visa, Diners, Amex, Eurocard, Mastercard.
           Bitters: Marstons Pedigree, Boddingtons, Trophy, Castle Eden, Best
                      Scotch.
           Lagers: Stella Artois, Gold Label, Heineken.

Examples of bar meals (lunchtime 6 days, evenings 7 days. Trad. Sun. lunch):
homemade steak pie, lasagne, scampi, seafood platter, gammon & pineapple, steaks, daily specials eg homemade cottage pie.
Examples of restaurant meals (every evening): *variety of steaks, half roast chicken, Dover sole.*

Pilgrims make their way to Egmanton church four times a year – there is said to have been a visitation by the Virgin Mary in the 18th century. Pilgrims of another kind make their way to 'Old Plough' (no definitive article) rather more than four times a year, for reasons more temporal than spiritual; namely good food and drink, and a rather agreeable atmosphere. Originally farmer's cottages, it became licensed in 1839, and has long been the meet of the annual Grove and Rufford hunt. Four cosy groundfloor rooms have a full quota of exposed beams and brickwork, nicely depicted by open log fires in winter. A recent addition is the upstairs steakbar restaurant, also beamed and with atmospheric subdued lighting. Brian and Audrey Wragg have, over seven years, established a faithful following. Children are welcome at lunchtime and early evening. Occasional barbecues. Darts, dominoes and quiz teams. No problem parking.

THE BOAT INN

Hayton, nr Retford.   Tel. (0777) 700158

Location: Main street, by canal.
Credit cards: Not accepted.
Accommodation: 3 singles, 6 twins, 2 doubles, one family, from £15 B & B.pp
Beers: Bass, Stones, guest.
Lagers: Carling, Warsteiner, Tennents Extra & LA.

Examples of bar/restaurant meals (lunch & evening, 7 days): *seafood au gratin, prawn & egg mayonnaise, garlic mushrooms; giant grill, steaks, bar-b-q spare ribs, turkey cordon bleu, salmon steak, gammon, carvery, salads, country lentil crumble, spinach & mushroom lasagne, vegetable chilli. Sweet trolley.*

There's always something happening here at this lively, friendly inn, run by Tony and Cath Railton. Amusing photographs around the walls and bedrooms with Nigerian names suggest a light-hearted approach. There's a regular quiz night, live entertainment and dominoes evenings, and do look out for the annual raft race on the Chesterfield Canal, always certain to be good damp fun. A high fence separates the canal from the superb children's play area. Inside is spacious and well-appointed, with four lounges and a separate restaurant (children welcome), and most suitable for a wedding reception or other special occasion. Food is taken seriously, though, and the carvery and steak grill are very popular. This is a pleasant area, and rooms very reasonable, so you could stay a while and work you way through the menu! Large car park.

THE BLACKSMITHS ARMS

Town Street, Clayworth, Retford.   Tel. (0777) 817348
            Location: Main street, village centre.
        Credit cards: Access, Visa.
    Accommodation: 9 doubles, all en suite (planning permission applied for).
              Bitters: Bass, Tetleys, Stones, guest.
               Lagers: Carling, Tennents Extra, Tennents LA.

Bar/restaurant meals (lunch & evening, 7 days): *local produce – fresh meat fish & poultry, vegetarian dishes. Homemade sweets.*

Major improvements and high standards have been the hallmark of Frank and Lucy Beales since they took over this 300-year-old former blacksmiths about three years ago. They specialise in fresh fish and homemade pies in the bar, and have a full a la carte and table d'hote in the restaurant. The 30 seater restaurant is attractively beamed with wagon wheels mounted on the walls. The lounge and locals' bar, with open fires, have been refurbished recently, and the low beams probably rattle a little on live jazz nights on the second and last Thursdays of each month. The third Thursday is reserved as quiz night. The new bedrooms, when available, will be well equipped, and a boon in an area short of good accommodation. This is a very pleasant little village in which to stay, on the banks of the Chesterfield Canal.

THE GRIFF INN

Drakeholes, nr Bawtry.   Tel. (0777) 817206
         Location: 10 mins from A1 at Blyth roundabout.
     Credit cards: Access, Visa.
   Accommodation: 3 dbls/twins (£50, £35 single). En suite, tv's, tea making.
          Bitters: Castle Eden, Tetley. Trophy Mild.
           Lagers: Skol, Stella Artois, Castlemaine, Heineken.

Examples of bar meals (lunch & evening, 7 days): *pies (eg steak & ale, game, seafood), liver & bacon casserole, pork & gammon hotpot, chicken breast with pineapple & banana sauce, steaks, lasagne, chilli, mussels in mustard & brandy sauce, shark steak with lemon & walnut sauce, halibut in cheese sauce, country lentil crumble, spicy vegetable casserole, harvesters pie, jacket potatoes, salads, ploughman's, sandwiches, daily specials, CARVERY.*
Examples of restaurant meals (as above): *avocado & oysters, Salamanca (Mexican dish with seafoods, ham & chicken), horn of plenty (pastry overflowing with prawns & scallops in creamy wine & ginger sauce), lamb noisettes in kiwi fruit sauce, special steaks, salmon & pineapple in puff pastry with Drambuie sauce, Chesterfield duck, vegetarian dishes. Trad. Sun. roasts from £4.25.*

The outstanding menu, a creative blend of the familiar and the exotic, would do credit to any top restaurant. Add to this the helpful staff and lovely location opposite the Chesterfield Canal and you will see why this 18th century inn is consistently rated by Egon Ronay and other major guides. With three tasteful bedrooms, individually decorated, one has the bonus of being able to enjoy it all again the next day! Weekends could be the best time, for landlord Michael Edmanson holds a Carvery and Dance (all ages) on Saturday evenings. Handy for Sherwood Forest, Clumber Park, Centre Parc, Doncaster etc.

THE CROSS KEYS

Main Street, Upton, Southwell.   Tel. (0636) 813269

     Location: On A612.
  Credit cards: Under review.
      Bitters: Marstons Pedigree, Boddingtons, Castle Eden, Batemans,
               guests
      Lagers: Stella Artois, Heineken, Dansk.

Examples of bar meals (lunch & evening, 7 days): *lamb casserole, lasagne verdi, Bombay cauliflower, stir fry, sausage & tuna hotpot, steak & mushroom pie, veg. goulash, fish pie, shepherds pie, crepes (savoury or sweet), ploughman's, French sticks.*
Examples of restaurant meals (evenings Thurs. – Sat., plus trad. Sun. lunch): *fresh salmon mousse, cheese & apple terrine; veal in orange & cointreau sauce, spinach & feta cheese (flavoured with dill & parsley topped with filo pastry), fish gumbo, porterhouse steak, dolmathes, cubes of beef (slowly cooked in honey, allspice, rosemary & red wine, with baby onions), chicken with shrimps & ginger in cream & wine sauce, fricasse of wild rabbit.*

A glance over the examples above will indicate that this is no ordinary pub. Wholesome and imaginative bar meals are chalked on a daily blackboard, while in the restaurant the choice is extensive and international, supplemented by a weekly gourmet menu. It need hardly be said that it is all prepared on the premises, and over the past eight years Mike and Kim Kirrage have established a formidable reputation, both with local people and major national guides, for the quality of their food. Mention should be made, too, of the unique upstairs restaurant, converted from a dovecote, light and airy with great high ceilings, and a super venue for a private party or wedding, perhaps. The two-tier bar is also rather pleasant, with open log fires, a tap room, a family area, and selection of good ales – a favourite subject of Mike's. Not one to be missed.

THE LAZY OTTER

Wyke Lane, Farndon, nr Newark.   Tel. (0636) 702416
Location: Riverside, ¹/₂ mile off A46.
Credit cards: Not accepted.
Bitters: Marstons Pedigree, Tetleys, Ansells, Burtons.
Lagers: Lowenbrau, Castlemaine, Skol.

Examples of bar meals (lunch & evening, except Sun. evening): *steaks, burgers, vegetable curry, macaroni & broccoli cheese, steak & kidney pie, West Indian chicken (thighs in tasty sauce), Yorkshire pudding with various fillings, curry, lasagne, moussaka, salads, jacket potatoes. Apple pie, gateau, trifle, cheesecake, two daily specials. Trad. Sun. roast.*

Just 15 yards from the river Trent, The Britannia (as it was formerly known), built in 1763, was frequented by barge operators. The new name came with a complete change of facilities. The front bar has retained the original arch brick fireplace, and the old oak beams are still supporting the two bars and separate dining room. Darts, dominoes and long alley skittles provide diversion, and Friday night is the time to be there if you like live entertainment. David, Eunice and Carol Hill have 40 years experience between them in running pubs, and have been establishing a following here over the last three years or so. They welcome children to the dining area or two beer gardens, where occasional barbecues are held. Besides parking for 100 cars, they have 45 yards of moorings on the river, and this is a great spot for sailing and fishing.

THE MAILCOACH REVIVED

Beaumond Cross, 13 London Road, Newark.   Tel. (0636) 605164

Location:	Town centre.
Credit cards:	Not accepted.
Accommodation:	2 singles, 2 doubles, one twin.
Bitters:	Benskins, Burtons, Tetleys, weekly guest(s).
Lagers:	Lowenbrau, Castlemaine, Skol.

Examples of bar meals (lunchtime only, Mon – Sat. Changed daily): 'Mail Coach' soup with crusty bread, Key West pecadillo (beef with olives & capers on bed of rice), vegetable crumble, pork in peanut sauce, Welsh faggots, cheese & nut loaf, ham & leek pie, loin of lamb with apricot & herb stuffing, stuffed herrings & mustard sauce, sausage & apple burgers, chicken in beer casserole, fresh-filled rolls, jacket potatoes. Lemon cream envelopes, sponge puddings, melon & ginger sorbet, cheesecake.

Vastly superior to the typical town pub, The Mail Coach is not 'a restaurant with beer', despite a daily menu quite exceptional in quality, variety and imagination. Rather the emphasis is on relaxation and friendliness – again, none too common in town pubs. Unbelievably, parts of it date back to around 1100, but mostly it is Georgian. It reverted to a public house only in 1989, reviving the name by which it was known c. 1811. Inside you will find prints from 1880, carpeted loung and bar, floor-boarded tap room, a solid oak bar, but no electronic games. David Kirrage and Lesley Alexander are the proprietors – David's family have been publicans in Newark since at least 1920. The private car park is small, but a public one is only 50 yards away.

THE BROWNLOW ARMS

High Marnham, Newark.   Tel. (0636) 821612

Location: Next to power station (take Sutton turn off A1).
Credit cards: Access, Visa.
Bitters: Theakstons Old Peculier, Greene King Abbott, Batemans, Boddingtons, Marstons Pedigree.
Lagers: Stella Artois, Heineken.

Examples of bar meals (lunch & evening, 7 days): *deep-fried venus clams served with mint & orange sauce, lamb Malaya, steak & mushroom pie, pork merango, baked swordfish, steaks, stir-fry chicken, mixed grill, lentil & hazelnut bake, ploughman's, sandwiches. Children's menu.*

Examples of restaurant meals (evenings only, Thurs. – Sun., plus trad. Sun. roasts): *smoked supreme of duck on hazelnut & raspberry vinaigrette (garnished with quail eggs); queen scallops (sauted with mushrooms, basil & truffles, flambed in cognac & cream), roast quail perfumed with rosemary on a Madeira & wild mushroom sauce, pork fillet stuffed with rich herb brie & tomato filling (on chive & Dijon mustard cream sauce), fillet steak.*

Don't be put off by the proximity to the power station: this is a very pleasant and peaceful spot (bit tricky to find, but do persevere), very close to the Trent, and not far from Sherwood Forest. It has come under new management recently, but continues to enjoy an excellent reputation for good, imaginative food. Monthly gourmet nights (eg Australian) make it even more interesting. Built in 1702 as a ferry inn, what is now a beautifully decorated restaurant and function room was a bunkhouse, whilst the horses slept underneath! Ask at the bar about a rather chilling tale of a bride who mysteriously disappeared here on her wedding night long ago, and seems to have returned by chance on an old photo. Besides the very comfortable three-room lounge, there's a public bar with pool and darts, a skittle alley and children's rooms. In 5 1/2 acres of grounds is a super play area with putting green, and barbecues are held.

THE BELL INN

Far Lane, Coleby, nr Lincoln.   Tel. (0522) 870240
           Location: In village, off A607.
       Credit cards: Visa, Mastercard.
            Bitters: Marston's Pedigree, Courage Directors, Tetley.
             Lagers: Lowenbrau, Castlemaine.

Examples of bar/restaurant meals (lunch & evening, 7 days): *charcoal grilled skillet of prawns, steaks, mixed grill, beefsteak & kidney pie, Chicken Kiev, swordfish steak in garlic butter, plaice Kiev, haddock, scampi, cold carvery, daily specials eg curries, roast rack of lamb with claret sauce, chicken en croute stuffed with smoked salmon & prawns, roast pork medallions with apricot & brandy sauce, vegetarian dishes. Children's menu Trad. Sun. roasts.*

Special mention must be made of the 'Around the World' daily selection, displayed on a board: chef likes to demonstrate his versatility in exotic cuisine from China, Indonesia, India, France and America. Conservative palates will be more than satisfied by the range of staple English favourites, such as succulent sugar and cider baked Lincolnshire ham. About 200 years old, the pub derives its name from its site on the field where the bell was cast for the village church. Part of it was a butcher's shop, and hooks can still be seen in the ceiling. A butcher hanged himself from one, and his spirit is said to be undeparted. Four open fires dipel any chill, and of special interest is an unusual collection of car number plates from around the world. Mick and Gail Aram are the affable hosts of 15 years standing. They welcome children but have no garden. Live jazz Friday evenings. Pool table. Large car park.

THE MARQUIS OF GRANBY

High Street, Wellingore.   Tel. (0522) 810442

Location:	Village centre.
Credit cards:	Access, Visa.
Accommodation:	2 twins, 1 family, all en suite, tv's, tea & coffee.
Bitters:	Youngers Scotch, IPA, Theakston's XB, McEwan's Export.
Lagers:	McEwans, Becks, Carlsberg.

Examples of bar/restaurant meals (lunch & evening, 7 days): *stuffed mushrooms, garlic prawns, salmon steak (with prawn, lobster & cream sauce), grilled whole lemon sole, steaks, duckling with black cherry sauce, beef in red wine with herb dumplings, steak & kidney pie, desperate Dan pie, fisherman's pie, chicken leek & ham pie, cashew & mushroom roast, gardener's pie, omelettes, salads, daily specials. Trad. Sun. roasts (booking advised).*

This is one of Lincolnshire's best known and reputed inns; the locals appear unanimous and enthusiastic in their praise. Credit must go to Ann and Martin Justice, whose dominion goes back 11 years. All meals are personally prepared by Ann and her team, no small task in view of the diversity and quality of the sizeable menu. Around 250 years old, the building is of attractive Lincolnshire stone, and replete in "olde worlde" splendour: exposed timbers, log fires and antique bottle collection. Pool, darts and dominoes provide indoor diversion, or take the benefit of the sun on the patio. Children are permitted at lunchtime if dining. A good base from which to visit Lincoln and its cathedral, Belton House, Fulbeck Hall and Craft Centre, Heritage Rooms at Navenby and many golf courses.

THE BEEHIVE

10/11 Castlegate, Grantham.   Tel. (0476) 67794
        Location: Town centre, near church.
    Credit cards: Not accepted.
         Bitters: Adnams Broadside & Southwold, guest.
          Lagers: Stella Artois, Heineken, Castlemaine.

Examples of bar meals (12 to 2pm, Mon – Sat): *Lincolnshire sausages, salads, jacket potatoes, sandwiches, ploughman's, blackboard specials eg steak & kidney pie, seafood platter, country pie, spiced lentil soup. Strawberry sorbet.* All homemade.

The only living pub sign in the country – a 200-year-old beehive – hangs outside this interesting town centre pub, under the tree where Cromwell is said once to have held council. It stands virtually in the very considerable shadow of St Wulfram's church, the third highest in the land. However, most customers come to enjoy good food and drink, in a most amenable atmosphere, under cheerful custodians John and Andrea Bull, in whose family the business has been for 30 years. Andrea does the cooking herself, and has earned a place in major national pub guides. One may enjoy it in either the public or lounge bar (with open fires) or in the walled garden to the rear. Draughts or scrabble are available for those who seek mental stimulation whilst imbibing. Handy for the shops, but parking no problem.

THE NAG'S HEAD

34 High Street, Heckington.   Tel. (0529) 60218
          Location: Village centre, by green.
       Credit cards: Access, Visa.
    Accommodation: 2 doubles, 1 fanily, all with tv & tea & coff. 2 with
                      private facilities. £22 single, £32 double.
           Bitters: Ruddles, Webster, Yorkshire.
            Lagers: Carlsberg, Fosters.

Examples of bar meals (lunch & evening, 7 days): *avocado & prawn hotpot, fresh salmon, steak & kidney pie, lasagne, fisherman's pie with garlic crumble top, prawns & cream cheese in puff pastry, game pie (shot by landlord!). Selection of sweets. Trad. Sun. roasts.*

The vast open spaces of the Lincolnshire Fens mean that good inns are relatively few and far between, but here's one surely worth seeking out, and which has found its way regularly into most of the main good pub guides. The A17 now bypasses the village, but this is still a very handily placed watering hole en route to the east coast. Local interest includes Spalding Flower Festival, Pearoom Craft Centre, and the only eight-sailed working windmill in the country, still producing flour every weekend in summer. The inn itself, built in 1684, is also alittle piece of history: Dick Turpin is said to have stayed here, apparently having relieved locals of their horses. Two lounge bars separated by an arch have open fires, original paintings by local artists and various antiques. The public bar has pool, and the restaurant is upstairs. Bruce and Gina Pickworth have spent nine years in making this such a local favourite, noted for good food on a menu revised daily. They welcome children, and have large garden to the rear. Free public car park adjacent.

THE RED LION

Newton, nr Sleaford.   Tel. (052 97) 256

Location:	1 mile south of A52, midway between Grantham & Donnington.
Credit cards:	Not accepted.
Accommodation:	6 rooms in s/c cottages, all en suite. £35 per room b & b. (under separate management).
Bitters:	Batemans, John Smiths.
Lagers:	Stella Artois, Carlsberg.

Examples of bar meals (lunch & evening, 7 days in summer): *cold carvery (renowned) eg fresh salmon, prawns, mackerel, sardines, pate, ox tongue, pork, homecured ham, stuffed chine, beef, turkey, salads. Hot carvery (choice of roast Fri & Sat evening, Sun lunch. Homemade puddings.*

Had you thought of Lincolnshire as like a billiard table, this picturesque and secluded little village, set in rolling wooded countryside, would disabuse of the notion. There are some lovely walks here, but be sure they all lead to The Red Lion, a common name for an uncommon pub, and one of the best known in these parts. It's of uncertain age but obviously fairly ancient, as witnessed by the mellow Lincolnshire stone and old timbers, adorned with period antiques and regalia. Modern luxuries are not to be spurned: in a separate wing two squash courts have whirlpool baths and are open to non-members at weekends. The accommodation is also of a high standard, and remarkably good value. But the good pub guides tend to focus on the superb carvery and salad bar – the landlord is a butcher by trade. Family rooms and garden with play area.

THE BULL

19 Market Place, Market Deeping, nr Peterboro'.   Tel. (0778) 343320
      Location: Town centre, junction of A15 with A16.
  Credit cards: Access, Visa.
       Bitters: Everard's Tiger, Old Original, Adnam's Best, guests.
        Lagers: Tudors, Red Stripe, Stella Artois.

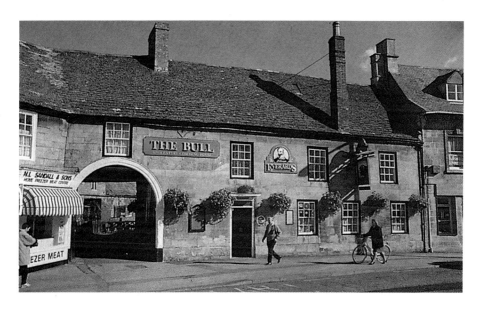

Examples of bar meals (lunchtime 7 days, Sat evening): *homemade lasagne, chilli, prawn & mushroom curry, steak & kidney pie, barbecued chicken, steaks, mixed grill, fisherman's platter, vegetable stir-fry, baked potatoes, sandwiches, daily specials. Children's menu. Trad. Sun. roasts.*

Nothing to do with four-legged bovines, the name refers to a Papal Bull, and the sign depicts historical Crowland Abbey, which is very close by. Built in 1585, the pub is replete with original timbers and stonework, full of little corridors and snug corners. Steps lead down to the remarkable 'Dugout', a low-ceilinged cellar where beer barrels stack behind the bar. Upstairs is the Woodhouse Room, which caters for private parties and can seat 32 in comfort. Off the lounge is the dining area, where one may partake of good, staple English fare at very modest prices. All this adds up to one of the most successful pubs in south Lincolnshire, a regular in major national guides, and a credit to landlord (for six years) David Dye. He welcomes children, and provides seating in the rear yard in summer. Special evenings monthly. Pool table. Car parking on market place.

THE CROWN INN

Debdale Hill, Old Dalby, nr Melton Mowbray.   Tel. (0664) 823134

Location: Off A46 Leicester to Newark road.
Credit cards: Not accepted.
Bitters: Adnam's Broadside, Woodforde's Wherry, Baldric & Nelson's Revenge, Tanglefoot, Bateman's XXXB, Marston's Pedigree & London Pride, Mauldens, Exmoor Gold, Mansfield – always 14 choices, direct from the wood.
Lagers: Carlsberg Export.

Examples of restaurant meals (lunch & evening, except Sun evening & all day Mon): *avocado with smoked lamb's tongue on yoghurt & mint coulis; entrecote with Colston Bassett stilton & port sauce, duck breast with sauce of lemon lime & champagne, fillets of sea bass with spring onion fresh ginger & wine sauce, daily specials. Sun. roasts Mother's Day or by request.*
Examples of bar meals (lunch & evening, except Sun evening): *black pudding & fried apple in cream of mustard sauce, homemade steak & kidney pie, lamb steak with raspberry sauce, sirloin steak, chicken Chinese style, seafood brochette on bed of crispy seaweed, pasta shells filled with crab cheese & spinach, kromeskies, sandwiches. Homemade puddings.*

With such a range of excellent ales, plus enormously rich and diverse menus, when it comes to choice this much celebrated 17th century inn can have few peers. Proprietors (for 10 years) Lynne Strafford Bryan and Salvatore Inguanta proudly proclaim the absence of microwaves, plastic or chips! As well as promoting local activities, they will always welcome strangers, and can readily accommodate private parties, small weddings and outside catering. Children are welcome, and the huge garden has petanque, croquet and large terrace. Les Routiers Pub of the Year 1991, and highly rated by every major guide.

THE ANCHOR INN FREEHOUSE

Walton-on-the-Wolds, nr Loughborough.   Tel. (0509) 880018
 Location: Village centre.
 Credit cards: Sorry, not accepted, but cheques with bankers' card are.
 Bitters: Burtons, Tetley, Ansell's Bitter & Mild. Guinness.
 Lagers: Lowenbrau, Castlemaine, Swan Light.

Examples of bar meals (lunch & evening, except Sun. evening): *prawn crab & apple cocktail, garlic mushrooms, chilli, award winning steak & kidney pie, herby fish pie, chicken Parisienne, Patricia's special lasagne, homecooked ham, homemade rabbit & pork pie, game pie, chicken Kiev, steaks, haddock, salmon & broccoli bake, scampi, salads, ploughman's, sandwiches, vegetarian dishes, daily homemade specials. Homemade bread & butter pudding, treacle & nut tart, award winning tipsy trifle.*

Numerous catering awards, proudly displayed on the walls, indicate that Patricia Shutt's cooking is rather special, a fact which has not escaped the attention of local people and journals, yet prices remain very reasonable. In the seven years since she and husband Leonard arrived, The Anchor has been an integral part of life in this delightful country village, and the famous Quorn Hunt meets here every Christmas Eve. The name was coined by locals in honour of Walton man Augustus Hampden, who became a real admiral in the last century. Superb models of ships are amongst the fascinating collections which serve the character of the single, large beamed lounge bar – stone jars, pewter mugs, brasses and copper, old prints, a Russian semavase (for making tea), and an old anchor of uncertain origin. Children are welcome in the large garden to front and rear.

THE STAG & HOUNDS

Burrough-on-the-Hill.   Tel. (0664 77) 375

           Location: Village centre.
        Credit cards: Not accepted.
             Bitters: 6 everchanging.
              Lagers: Lowenbrau, Skol.

Examples of bar meals (every evening, Sat & Sun lunch): *Stag & Hounds smokies (smoked mackerel & Melton Mowbray stilton cheese sauce), drunken bull (prime beef chunks in beer), steaks, homemade pies, ploughman's, sandwiches, daily specials. Stag Ice (homemade cherry & coconut icecream in chocolate shell, with grenadine). Trad. Sun. roasts £6.30 (reductions for children).*

Prince Edward and Mrs Simpson often stayed in the village, and the story goes that they called here for a drink. But they had no money on them, and the landlord, refusing to believe their identity, turfed them out! Perhaps it is his spirit that lingers on, drinking beer and turning on music, still rueing his colossal blunder! His successors since July 1988, Sue and Pete Ierston are rather more welcoming, and take pride in serving homecooked food and quality beers, winning accolades from CAMRA, plus a place in major good pub guides. Their 16th century pub has its quota of exposed timbers, brickwork and fireplaces, and a small collection of beer mats and pump clips. A pool table and quiz machine provide diversion, and there's live music every Thursday. Children are welcome if well behaved in the games room, and the garden has play equipment and wooden house. Car park.

THE KING'S ARMS

Top Street, Wing, Oakham. Tel. (0572) 85315

Location: A6003, Uppingham to Oakham road.
Credit cards: Access, Visa.
Accommodation: 2 doubles, 2 twins, en suite.
Beers: Bass, Ruddles, Worthington.
Lagers: Carling, Tennents Extra.

THE KINGS ARMS ... WING

Examples of bar/restaurant meals (lunch & evening 7 days, except Sunday evenings in winter): *turkey curry, lasagne, drunken bull pie, grilled halibut steak, homemade steak & kidney pie, gaelic steak, pheasant in red wine & port sauce. Selection of sweets. Cold carvery restaurant.*

It is believed that penitents used to crawl around the famous Wing Maze (a circle of turf, not the Hampton Court variety), to the jeers of onlookers. Thirsty and disoriented, they would have been grateful for this welcoming traditional 17th century inn. Being in a conservation area, great care was taken in recent refurbishment not to spoil character features like the exposed stonework or open fires. Welcome additions are the separate cold carvery restaurant (to supplement an already very good reputation for food) housed in the adjoining old village bakehouse, and four bedrooms, complete with colour TV's, tea and coffee facilities and hair dryers. Marie and Richard Belton welcome well-behaved children, and of course tourists, who are well placed here for Rutland Water, Oakham Castle and other attractions.

THE OLD PLOUGH FREEHOUSE

1 Church Street, Braunston-in-Rutland.   Tel. (0572) 722714
                                            Fax. (0572) 770382

          Location: 2 miles south west of Oakham.
      Credit cards: Access, Visa, Diners, Amex, Switch.
           Bitters: Courage Directors & Best, Theakstons, Adnams, guests.
            Lagers: Becks, Fosters, Miller.

Examples of bar meals (lunch & evening, 7 days): *chicken stuffed with lobster & prawns inlobster sauce, steaks, slices of black pudding cooked in Scrumpy Jack cider, fresh salmon stuffed with prawns wrapped in filo pastry on fish yourt sauce, filllet of sole stuffed with crabmeat in lobster & cream sauce, steak kidney & Guinness pie, fresh pasta dishes, stilton & walnut pate, the famous "Plough Crusty", vegetarian dishes. Pavlova with fresh fruit, death by chocolate. Trad. Sun. roasts.*

One is well advised to book a table here, for Andrew and Amanda Reid, together with chef Nick Quinn, have rapidly acquired a first class reputation for tantalising menus (changed every eight weeks) and a very special atmosphere. High standards of hygiene and provision of healthy food recently secured the 'Heartbeat Award'. An old coaching inn of uncertain age, The Plough captures the very spirit of Rutland, in rolling hunting country. The largest horseshoe in England's smallest county is mounted in the garden, but oriental umbrellas hanging in the conservatory dining room add a cosmopolitan touch. Red letter days are celebrated throughout the year, with appropriate menus and entertainment. Darts, dominoes and quizzes provide other indoor amusement, while outside is petanque and summer barbecues. Children welcome. Car park.

THE DOG & HEDGEHOG INN

Dadlington, nr Nuneaton.　　　　　　　　　　　　　Tel. (0455) 212629

Location:　3 miles north west of Hinckley.
Credit cards:　Not accepted.
Bitters:　Brew 11, Bass.
Lagers:　Carling, Tennents.

Examples of bar meals (lunchtime Mon – Fri): *turkey cordon bleu, omelettes, salads, lasagne, selection of fish, steak & kidney pie, ploughman's. Children's menu.*
Examples of restaurant meals (lunch & evening, Tues – Sat): *steaks (speciality), mixed grill, gammon, roast chicken, beef bourgignon, selection of fish incl. salmon, salads. Gateaux, trifle. Special coffees.*

The only pub so named in Britain was once a malthouse for brewing, and beer has been served here for 300 years. The building has been extensively altered and heightened, with a feature balcony for extra seating. The old cottage next door is now the restaurant, and with an overflow room upstairs one can usually be sure of a seat, to enjoy one of the steaks which are the popular speciality. The village is small but very pretty, and the inn backs on to open fields, affording lovely views. Bosworth Battlefield and Ashby canal are very close. Chris and Lucy Halliday are your genial hosts, who welcome children and provide them with a play area in the garden.

THE COUNTRYMAN

23 Leicester Road, Sharnford.   Tel. (0455) 272268
        Location: Village centre.
    Credit cards: Not accepted.
        Bitters: Everards Tiger, Ruddles County, John Smith.
        Lagers: Carlsberg, Carlsberg Export, Fosters.

Examples of bar meals (lunch & evening, 7 days): *lamb tikka marsala, beef Bourgignonne, butterfly pork, chicken chasseur, lasagne, homemade pies (eg steak & kidney, steak & stilton, chicken & vegetable, game), steaks & grills, chilli, curry, trout & almonds, plaice, omelettes, salads, jacket potatoes, vegetarian dishes, sandwiches, daily specials. Trad. Sun. roasts.*

For a measure of the degree in which pub food has improved in recent years, this 18th century inn is a splendid example. Licensees Alan and Sallyanne Lawson consult with chef David to create well thought out and diverse menus, a satisfying blend of succulent homegrown and international dishes, all prepared on the premises, of course. But if you're just calling in for a drink, you will receive the same friendly greeting, and the middle bar is set aside just for drinkers. The Lounge is for eating and the Public has darts and dominoes, and all are well furnished and comfortable. Children are welcome, and the garden has a play area and barbecue. Large car park opposite pub.

THE PLOUGH INN

Littlethorpe.   Tel. (0533) 862383
        Location: Village centre, 7 miles south west of Leicester.
    Credit cards: Access, Visa, Mastercard, Eurocard.
         Bitters: Everard's Old Original, Tiger, Beacon, Adnams, guest.
          Lagers: Stella Artois, Carlsberg Export, Tuborg.

Examples of bar/restaurant meals (lunch & evening, 7 days): *steak & kidney pie, chilli, hunter's steak, chicken chasseur, plaice stuffed with prawns & mushrooms, trout, veg lasagne, cheese & mushroom flan, daily specials. Fruit crumble, treacle tart, death by chocolate. Trad. Sun. roasts.*

Every village should have its traditional friendly local, and The Plough fulfills the role commendably. If you care to rub shoulders with the 'natives', perhaps over a game of skittles or darts, they will tell you that the beer is very drinkable and the food always of a consistently high standard, courtesy of Stuart and Christine Steedman, who've spent the last 10 years or so here. 16th century and half-thatched, the pub lacks not for atmosphere, being well timbered, with a good brass collection and much admired tapestries in the dining room. Special dates, such as Beaujolais, New Year, Christmas etc do not pass unnoticed. Children are welcome inside, ut there is a patio with sunshades (see photo). Skittle alley doubles as function room. Ample parking.

39

THE LORD BASSETT ARMS

4 Leicester Road, Sapcote.   Tel. (0455) 272394

Location:	Village centre.
Credit cards:	Not accepted.
Accommodation:	2 doubles, 2 twins.
Bitters:	Adnams, Beacon, Tiger.
Lagers:	Tuborg, Stella Artois.

Examples of bar/restaurant meals (12 to 3pm, 7 to 9pm, 7 days): *crispy coated vegetables with dip, lemon sole in white wine & mushroom sauce, chicken briev, steak & kidney pie, chicken ham & leek pie, beef & venison pie, mixed grill, steaks, lasagne, veg lasagne. Sunday roasts only by arrangement.*

For all the turmoil there has been in the pub trade in recent years, it is gratifying to know that the likes of The Lord Bassett are still holding their own. The regulars keep returning for that bonhomie which is the essence of the traditional village local. There is no doubt that the vital spark comes from the licensees, in this case Ron and Chris Pappin, who've provided the hospitality at this 18th century inn for the last 16 years – eons by today's standards. Good cheer is extended to passers by, who often pull off the A5 or M69 for good food and refreshment. They find themselves in one of two cosy timbered bars (or dining room), with panelled walls and the ubiquitous brasses. Entertainment comes in the form of darts, dominoes and table skittles, and there's also a skittle alley which doubles as a function room. Children are welcome and have a see-saw in the garden. New accommodation added recently.

YE OLDE BULL'S HEAD

Main Street, Broughton Astley.   Tel. (0455) 282343
        Location: Village centre, junction of Cosby Road and B581.
   Credit cards: Not accepted.
         Bitters: Everards Traditional, Tiger, Beacon, Old Original, guests.
         Lagers: Stella Artois, Carlsberg.

Examples of bar meals (lunchtime Mon – Sat, evenings Tues – Sat, plus Bank Hols): *homemade steak & kidney pie, cottage pie, lasagne, chilli, curry, steak, burgers, scampi, vegetarian lasagne, hot cobs, ploughman's, salads. Children's menu.*

November 5th is a day to remember: the bonfire and firework display held on the field to the rear of the pub is renowned locally. The same field is used by travelling fairs in spring and autumn, and for car boot ales, Sunday markets and other activities. High summer is the best season in which to enjoy the garden, with banks of flowers and a stream populated by ducks. This stream used to flood regularly, carrying away barrels of beer (and making somebody's day, no doubt), until work was done to prevent it. Geoff and Linda Stokes took charge of their 19th century pub about four years ago, and carried out refurbishment and redecoration to both bars. Of special note is a wall in the lounge built with bricks and bottles. There's as much indoor activity as outdoor: pool, darts, skittles, quiz nights, 60's nights, karaoke and special promotions. Barbecues arranged, weather permitting. Family room and play area. Ample parking. Rated by national good pub guide.

THE CHEQUERS COUNTRY INNE

Main Street, Ullesthorpe, nr Lutterworth.

Tel. (0455) 209214
Fax. (0455) 209144

Location: Village centre, on B577.
Credit cards: Access, Visa, Amex, Switch.
Accommodation: 2 singles, 4 doubles, 5 twins, 3 family. All en suite with tv's, tea & coffee, trouser presses, direct phones, hair driers.
Bitters: Theakston's Best, XB, Old Peculier, guest.
Lagers: Becks, McEwans.

Examples of bar meals (lunch & evening, 7 days): *homemade chicken supreme with stilton & leek sauce, 'Old Peculier' pie, chicken Kiev, curry, steaks, lasagne, vegetarian crumble, salads, sandwiches, daily specials.*
Examples of restaurant meals (lunch & evening, except Sun evening): *steak Diane, escalope of veal in brandy & cream sauce, pork chop with juniper, fillet steaaks stuffed with stilton & wrapped in bacon, crispy half duckling with orange & brandy sauce. Trad. Sun. roasts.*

Near the Roman centre of England, where Fosse Way meets Watling Street, this former farmhouse (dating 'only' from 1721) is superbly placed for access to most everywhere (including NEC), but food and accommodation are of a standard undreamt of by the Romans! Freshly refurbished, the well equipped bedrooms are reasonably priced (ask about weekend rates). The two bars and restaurant are truly "olde worlde", with no less than five interconnecting rooms. There's also a family room, and children have their own menu, plus swings in the large garden (with barbecue, tables and chairs). A marquee seats 150 and is ideal for weddings etc. A most commendable inn, personally run by father and son, Neville and Gary Thomas.

THE OLDE ROYAL OAK

Valley Lane, Bitteswell. Tel. (0455) 552406
<blockquote>
Location: Village centre, 2 miles from jncn 20 of M1.
Credit cards: Not accepted.
Bitters: Davenports, Tennents.
Lagers: Castlemaine, Labatts, Carlsberg Export.
</blockquote>

Examples of bar meals (lunch & evening, except Sun evening): *steaks (rib eye a speciality), fresh fish (eg lemon sole, salmon, Dover sole), chicken breast Cajun style, homemade steak & kidney pie, chicken pie, tagliatelle with ham & mushrooms, vegetarian dishes, sandwiches, daily specials. Homemade fruit pies, trifles. Trad. Sun. roasts (booking advised).*

It is encouraging to know that in these troubled times good village pubs are still thriving, providing a focal point for the community spirit. A number of local associations meet here at this 16th century relief coaching inn, and the many regulars mingle with visitors to enjoy the first rate facilities and wholesome home cooking (rated by the brewery's good food guide). Both bars (one a snug) are beamed and tastefully furnished, and the lounge has an open fire. Table skittles, darts and dominoes are the source of much jocularity and friendly competition, and the occasional summer barbecue is also good fun. Arthur and Maureen Bird have hosted for over 11 years. They are pleased to accommodate chidren in the family room – there's also a garden. Bitteswell is a pleasant village with an interesting church.

THE WHITE SWAN

Main Street, Shawell.   Tel. (0788) 860357

Location:	Village centre, 1 mile off A5.
Credit cards:	Visa, Mastercard, Eurocard.
Bitters:	Theakstons Old Peculier & XB, ABC Best, Tetley, Burton, Shipston.
Lagers:	Labatts, Lowenbrau, Carlsberg.

Examples of bar/restaurant meals (lunch & evening, 7 days): *breast of chicken supreme filled with stilton & covered with creamy leek & bacon sauce, homemade lasagne, fish pie, curry, steak, fillet of salmon on asparagus sauce, speciality fish day on Thursdays. Trad. Sun. roasts.*

Many might wish they had a local such as this in their own village. As the photo shows, it is most pleasing on the eye, likewise inside, with lovley old wood panelling, beams, brickwork and fireplace. Built around 1700, the bar has changed very little, so retains all the period character and a remarkable atmosphere. A games room (pool, darts and skittles) and a restaurant have been added, and cuisine is well above average pub fare, as the examples above would suggest. The menus are changed regularly, and in summer a pig roast in the large garden is a popular event. Proprietors Sharon and David Hill also keep a good range of beers and, more important, a warm welcome for regulars and visitors, including children. Functions may be held in the dining room. Large car park.

THE BLACK HORSE

94 Main Street, Foxton.   Tel. (085 884) 250

Location: Top of village, 2 miles off A6.
Credit cards: Not accepted.
Accommodation: 1 double, 2 twins, with shower, tv, tea & coffee.
Bitters: Marston's Best & Pedigree, Border Mild.
Lagers: Heineken, Stella Artois.

Examples of bar meals (lunchtime Mon – Sat, filled rolls on Sunday): *homemade steak & kidney pie, chilli, lasagne verdi, vegetarian dishes, ploughman's, sandwiches, daily specials.*
Examples of restaurant meals (lunch & evening Mon – Sat, plus trad. Sun. lunch)*: steaks (incl. 16ozs T-bone), chicken Kiev, halibut in lobster & prawn sauce, lamb in orange & ginger, cashew nutballs in mushroom sauce. Mississippi mud pie, raspberry & redcurrant pie.*

The famous Foxton Locks are very close by, and many boaters come ashore to savour the pleasures of this old pub, which appears in the Inland Waterways Guide. However you arrive, you are assured of a friendly reception from David and Jenny Quelch, now in their fifth year here. The original part comprises of two bars; the cosy local and larger lounge, comfortably furnished and with a real fire. Special mention must go to the 50-seater conservatory restaurant (used also for functions) added three years ago, and to the large, very well kept garden (and play area), with lovely views. A barbecue is available for private hire. Indoor amusements are in the form of darts, dominoes and long alley skittles, and there's live jazz every Wednesday. Children welcome. Large car park.

THE THORNHILL ARMS

Station Road, Rushton.   Tel. (0536) 710251

Location:	Village centre.
Credit cards:	Access, Visa.
Accommodation:	1 single, 1 twin, 2 family. Tv's, tea & coffee.
Bitters:	Ruddles, Websters, guest.
Lagers:	Carslberg, Fosters, Holsten.

Examples of bar/restaurant meals (lunch & evening, except Sun evening): *homemade steak & kidney pie, chilli, curry, roast lamb/beef, steaks, pasta dishes, lemon sole, scampi, salmon steak with parsley sauce, vegetarian lasagne, daily specials. Trad. Sun. roasts.*

"The Rose of the Shires", as Northamptonshire likes to call itself, is distinguished by a style of stone construction not unlike that in the Cotswolds, of which this 300-year-old farmhouse is a prime example. Every bit as stalwart as they look, the exposed stone walls combine with the solid timbers (look for interesting animal carvings) and inglenook to create a very pleasant environment. Indeed, resident ghost 'Charlie' seems reluctant to leave. Landlords for the last three years or so, Brian Barnicoat and Gary Moscow are pleased to offer a good range of homecooked food on everchanging menus. Whilst enjoying it, one can rest one's gaze over an expansive view of the cricket ground and countryside from one of the bars or, better still, from the large garden. Children welcome. Darts.

THE STAR INN

2 Bridge Street, Geddington, nr Kettering.   Tel. (0536) 742386
          Location: Village centre, 1/2 mile off A43.
    Credit cards: Access, Visa.
          Bitters: Ruddles Best & County, Websters, guest.
          Lagers: Carlsberg, Holsten.

Examples of bar meals (lunch & evening, 7 days): *homemade chicken casserole & herb dumplings, Cheshire lamb crumble, beef beer & bacon pie, seafood crepes, rib-eye steak platter, lentil moussaka, broccoli & nut pilaff, salads, daily specials.*
Examples of restaurant meals (as above): *half honey roasted duck in apricot & brandy sauce, lamb Shrewsbury, Paul's special (beef fillet filled with rich pate, in puff pastry, port wine sauce), fillet of plaice filled with lobster in thermidor sauce, farmhouse cobbler (chucky vegetables in stilton sauce, topped with herb scones), leek roulade, grills. Trad. Sun. roasts.*

As the photo shows, the pub stands at the foot of the Eleanor Cross, one of 12 built to commemorate Eleanor of Castile, wife of Edward I, who died in the 12th century. Three only remain, this the best preserved. This pleasant village is also distinguished by an appealing 17th century pub, run by Paul and Michele Boddington for the last two years or so. They have obviously taken great pains over the sizeable menus; it's all homecooked and caters for every palate, but will not damage your wealth. The two bars and separate dining room want not for character. Darts and skittles are played, and there's also a function room. A warm welcome is extended to children. No garden. Small car park to rear.

THE BELL

Little Addington, nr Kettering.   Tel. (0933) 651700

Location:	Village centre, off A604 6 miles from Kettering.
Credit cards:	Access, Visa.
Bitters:	Adnams, Marston's Pedigree, Hook Norton, Tetley, John Bull, guest.
Lagers:	Lowenbrau, Castlemaine, Kronenbourg, Dansk LA.

Examples of bar meals (lunch & evening, 7 days): *steaks (speciality), mixed grill, spicy sausages, salmon steak with prawn & cucumber sauce, chef's hot seafood platter, tuna steak, whole snapper in lemon sauce, mixed veg. crumble, broccoli & cream cheese pie, daily specials.*
Examples of restaurant meals (as above, except Sat lunchtime): *banana stuffed breast of chicken with rum sauce, mixed fish kebab, red mullet Nicoise, well-hung prime steaks, mixed bean casserole, nut & vegetable biryani. Trad. Sun. roasts.*
NB Special price over 60's menu Mon. & Sun. lunchtime (except Bank Hols).

Proprietors Ros and William Franks are especially proud of their top quality Scottish beef, which is hung to mature on the premises. But the rest of their comprehensive menus is equally mouthwatering, fresh fish and vegetarian dishes being well represented. For even more variety keep a watch out for theme evenings, like German or Italian, with appropriate music and wine. Yet prices remain very fair, and this plus the warmth of the hospitality draws custom from miles around. The building dates from 1666, and an early morning ghost is said to flit between the old stone walls, beams and fireplace in the three lounges. The separate restaurant can accommodate small weddings or other functions. Garden, large car park.

THE OLD RED LION

12 The Green, Clipston, nr Market Harborough.   Tel. (085 886) 257

Location: Village centre, on B4036.
Credit cards: Not accepted.
Bitters: Charles Wells Eagle & Bombardier, guest. Riding dark mild.
Lagers: Red Stripe, Kellerbrau.

Examples of bar meals (lunch & evening 7 days, except Tues in winter): *homemade soup, Chinese dim sums, steaks, mixed grill (noted), steak & kidney pie, Lancashire hotpot, lasagne, Avonshire pork chop, salmon steak with choice of sauces, whole trout with herbs or garlic, vegetarian dishes, snacks, daily specials. Trad. Sun. roasts.*

'Headquarters' of the village cricket team and clay pigeon shoot, home to league pool and darts teams, this 16th century coaching house is naturally the focal point of village social life. Like all the best locals, however, its doors are always equally open to visitors – no cliques here. Licensees Kenneth and Jacky Pickles, themsleves relative newcomers, like to see new faces, and tailor their menu to accommodate a broad range of palates. Children are welcome, and a notable feature of the large garden (where barbecues are a popular summer draw) is the play area, but the youngsters will also take to the mini menagerie and aviary. That may whet the appetite for a visit to nearby Naseby Battlefield, and Lamport Hall is also an easy drive. Large car park.

THE FITZGERALD ARMS

Naseby, nr Northampton   Tel (0604) 740273

          Location: 1/2 mile off A50.
      Credit cards: Not accepted.
           Bitters: Bass, 2 guests.
            Lagers: Carling, Tennents Extra.

Examples of bar meals (lunch & evening, not Mon lunchtime except Bank Hols):
*steak & kidney pie, game pie, chicken mushroom pie, beef Wellington, mixed grill (noted),
steaks, chicken Kiev, trout, scampi, haddock, vegetable lasagne, deep fried vegetable
platters, salads, large rolls, Trad.Sun. roasts.*

Value for money is more important than ever in current straitened times, and the
Fitzgerald Arms is well regarded for just that – both food and beers are keenly
priced, portions generous (the mixed grill, especially, is not for the faint hearted).
This early Victorian pub is also distinguished by having the source of the River
Avon, an old well, in its large garden. Inside, you will discover two bars, both
imbued with friendly warmth. The aptly named 'Grunters' or Public bar is where
the locals gather, under the gaze of numerous framed pictures of old boars and
porkers. Scenes of hunting and the Civil War (Battle of Naseby Monument and
Museum are very near) are to be found in the Lounge, warmed by an open fire. A
further games room houses skittles and darts. Children welcome. Large car park.

THE RED LION

52 Main Road, Crick.   Tel. (0788) 822342
            Location: Village centre, ³/4 mile off M1 junction 18.
         Credit cards: Not accepted.
              Bitters: Traditional – Ruddles Best, Webster's Yorkshire, Hook Norton.
               Lagers: Carlsberg, Fosters, Holsten.

Examples of bar meals (lunch & evening, except Sundays) lunchtime: *homemade steak & kidney pie, sirloin steak, chicken & broccoli bake, plaice, scampi, vegetarian dishes; evening: roast duckling with apple sauce, chicken Kiev, fillet steak, rainbow trout, vegetarian dishes.*

Less than a mile from the turmoil of the M1, this agreeable 17th century coaching inn makes for a pleasant halt (infinitely better than a motorway stop), and is worth an excursion in itself. The first recorded landlord was in 1766, but for the last 12 years that position has been occupied by Tom and Mary Marks, who extend an exceptionally warm greeting to all (including children over 14). Mary's steak & kidney pie is much sought after, but there are ample alternatives (14 items at lunchtime), served with fresh vegetables. The digestion is aided by comfortable, old-fashioned surroundings: exposed timbers, stone walls, open fires. No electronic howlings are allowed to disturb the peace. Small garden nd terrace. Large car park. Althorpe House 10 miles away.

THE ARNOLD ARMS

2 Ware Road, Barby, nr Rugby. Tel. (0788) 891403

Location: Village centre, 1¹/₂ miles off A5.
Credit cards: Not accepted.
Bitters: Theakston's Old Peculier, Ruddles County, Websters Yorkshire.
Lagers: Holsten, Carlsberg, Fosters.

Examples of bar/dining room meals (lunch & evening, Mon – Sat): *prawn cocktail, garlic mushrooms, homemade steak & kidney pie, venison in red wine sauce, steaks, lasagne, plaice, scampi, trout, vegetarian dishes, daily specials. Selection of sweets. Trad. Sun. roasts (noted).*

The English village is still much to be admired (let's face it, many of our big towns are awful), and the cornerstone of village social life remains the traditional village inn. The Arnold Arms is one such, and Phillip Headley and Peter Maddison, who took over in 1990, aim to keep it that way. They continue to serve staple English pub favourites in an atmosphere of genuine bon homie, to be partaken of in either dining room or two bars, warmed by open fires. Prices are very moderate, and Sunday lunch is regarded as particularly good value. Darts, table skittles and pool provide indoor diversion, but in kind weather why not stretch the legs and take a pleasant stroll to the canals either side of the village. Children are welcome, and have a playground in the garden.

YE OLDE SARACEN'S HEAD

Little Brington.   Tel. (0604) 770640
      Location: Village centre, 3 miles off junction 16 of M1.
  Credit cards: Not accepted.
       Bitters: Ruddles Best, Websters, Triple Crown.
       Lagers: Holstein, Carlsberg, Fosters.

Examples of bar meals (lunch & evening, 7 days): *homemade soup, sirloin steak, farmhouse grill, lasagne, faggots, plaice, cod, haddock, scampi, spicy potato wedges with dip, homemade steak & kidney pie, macaroni cheese, cauliflower cheese with hot crusty bread, salads, ploughman's, sandwiches, daily specials. Fruit crumble, hot fudge cake, liqueur icecream.*

If you should happen by on a Sunday evening, join the locals in a sing-along to the accompaniment of landlady Betty Dodds on the organ. It is in such spirit that she and husband Cyril have, over 14 years, made their cosy, unspoilt 17th century pub the hub of social life in this typical Northants village, and a popular halt for visitors on the way to nearby Althorp House. Many will be grateful for the new tearooms in the old barn, charmingly in the style of the Victorian era. Good food and beer have won recognition from leading naitonal guides, and it is the steaks and farmhouse grill which are the perennial favourites. A magnificent collection of memorabilia may be seen in the two timbered bars, warmed by open fires. Pool, darts, skittles and dominoes. Well-behaved children permitted, and garden has an aviary. Organist on Saturday evenings.

THE WHITE HART INN

80 Main Road, Hackleton.   Tel. (0604) 870271

Location: Village centre.
Credit cards: Not accepted.
Bitters: Theakston's XB, Ruddles Best, Websters.
Lagers: Carlsberg, Fosters, Holstein.

Examples of bar meals (lunch & evening, except Sundays): *homemade steak &*
kidney pie with Ruddles ale, fried haddock fillet in Yorkshire bitter batter, steak platter,
chicken Kiev, salmon & prawns in creamy seafood sauce, scampi, lasagne, deep fried
prawn fritters, savoury spinach & cheese pancake, vegetarian dishes, salads, ploughman's,
sandwiches, daily specials. Blackboard pudding menu. Fresh rolls on Sundays.

Character, that most elusive of qualities in a pub, is to be found here in abundance.
Pride of place should perhaps go to the old well in one of the bars, but there's also a
splendid inglenook festooned with all sorts of antiquarian oddities, and ofcourse the
customary exposed timbers and brickwork. It's all immaculately well kept, and
would be familiar to the very first landlord, recorded in 1739. Present incumbents
are Richard and Penny French, who care very much about good food and
atmosphere – always extra lively when skittles and darts are played. Children are
welcome in the lounge if accompanied by adults who are dining, but otherwise
there's a large garden with plenty of seating and a paddock. Large car park.

FIVE BELLS

14 Church Lane, Bugbrooke.   Tel. (0604) 832483
            Location: Village centre, opp. church, 2 miles off junction 16 of M1.
       Credit cards: Not accepted.
             Bitters: Websters, Yorkshire, Ruddles, Courage, guest.
             Lagers: Fosters, Carlsberg, Holsten Export.

Examples of bar meals (lunch & evening, 7 days): *selection of steaks (incl. giant 32 or 48ozs!), fresh fish of day, seafood platter, giant gammon steak (14 or 28ozs), salads, daily specials eg lemon sole with crabmeat & scallops, plaice fillets filled with prawns & mushrooms, kyden chicken, steak & prawns, vegetarian dishes, salads.*

An unbelievable 3lb rump steak would surely defeat even the most ravenous appetite, but no doubt some have managed it, and if not there's always the doggy bag! A 28ozs gammon steak also beggars belief, so this is clearly not a place for the faint-hearted. Ofcourse there are more modestly sized dishes to tickle the palate, and prices are extraordinarily reasonable, including wines. Not surprisingly, a new extension has been added, principally as an eating area. The pub was built around 1700, and takes its name from the bells of the church opposite, constructed around the same time. There's one timbered public bar and two lounges (children welcome). An area with an open fire is set aside for pool, skittles and darts. A large garden has a patio (barbecues held in summer), swings and slides. Parking for 70 cars. Karen and Stephen Allen are the generous hosts.

THE FOX INN

Baker Street, Farthinghoe, nr Brackley.   Tel. (0295) 710393

Location: Village centre, 4 miles from Brackley.
Credit cards: Not accepted.
Bitters: Charles Wells Eagle & Bombadier.
Lagers: Red Stripe, Kellerbrau.

The Fox
Farthinghoe

Examples of bar meals (lunch & evening, 7 days): *homemade beef & stout pie, chilli, beef Wellington, steaks, roast duckling, plaice, rainbow trout, lemon sole, vegetable lasagne, vegetable au gratin, nut roast Portuguese, daily specials. Children's meals. Trad. Sun. roasts.*

The local parachute club likes to 'drop by' at this friendly 16th century local, as do the flying and gliding clubs, but it is equally amenable to those of us stuck on terra firma. Regulars unselfishly welcome visitors, as do proprietors David and Barbara Warburton, of course. They have completely refurbished their Lounge bar to seat 36 in comfort, while the Public bar, warmed by a wood fire, provides darts, dominoes and shove ha'penny. The cooking is very well reputed, the beef and stout pie being a particular favourite, and menus are revised periodically. Children are also made welcome, and the large garden has swing, Aunt Sally pitch and barbecue (parties catered for – min. booking 10, max 40). One is well placed for an excursion to the Cotswolds (20 mins) or Silverstone (15 mins). Car park.

WEST MIDLANDS

Kenilworth Castle, form watercolour by David Cox.

THE AXE & COMPASS

Wolvey Heath, Wolvey, nr Hinckley.   Tel. (0455) 220240

     Location: 1 mile south of A5, near M69 junction.
Credit cards: Access, Visa, Diners, Amex.
      Bitters: Bass, Highgate Mild, guests.
       Lagers: Tennents, Tennents Extra, Carling.

Examples of bar meals (lunch & evening, 7 days): *homemade beef & Guinness pie, chicken & prawn Indienne, seafood tagliatelle, Lancashire hotpot, ravioli Bolognese with garlic croutons, steak, pizza, cheese & vegetable hotpot, omelettes, ploughman's, sandwiches.*
Examples of restaurant meals (lunch & evening, except Sun. evening): *calves' liver & raspberry vinaigrette, mushrooms in stilton & chive sauce, salmon & sea bream with asparagus & white wine sauce, paella Valencia, best end of lamb with plum coulis, medallions of beef marchand de vin, veal stroganoff. Trad. Sun. roasts.*

Around 50 alternatives are chalked up daily on a blackboard in the bar, in addition to the considerable restaurant menu (further enhanced by special gourmet evenings), affording a quite amazing variety of choice which can have few equals. This is only possible due to the pride the Jones family take in their business: Robert and Julia provide the hospitality, son David is head chef and daughter Samantha is the restaurant manageress. Built as recently as 1933, their country inn is nevertheless timber beamed and panelled, comfortably upholstered and with open log fires. The lounge seats 100, the restaurant 36. The latter doubles as a function room, but a two-acre field is available for outdoor activities. Children are welcome, and have a play area in the large garden.

THE PHEASANT

Withybrook, nr Coventry.   Tel. (0455) 220480
        Location: Next to brook running thro' village.
   Credit cards: Access, Visa, Mastercard.
        Bitters: Courage Directors, John Smith, Dark mild.
        Lagers: Hofmeister, Fosters, Kronenbourg.

Examples of bar meals (lunch & evening, 7 days): *braised liver & onions, faggots, curry, steak & kidney pie, quiches, venison pie, braised pheasant, braised guinea fowl, omelettes, steaks & grills, baked haddock or cod, fisherman's pie, ploughman's. Treacle sponge pudding, chocolate finger eclair, Bavarian apple flan.*
Examples of restaurant meals (lunch & evening, 7 days)*: scampi pernod, lobster thermidor, steak au poivre, braised gammon (in honey, cider apple & cream sauce), vegatarian goulash, red dragon pie, broccoli & walnut lasagne. Rum ba-ba, cheesecake, chocolate fudge cake.*

Nicely situated by a brook, The Pheasant affords a pleasant waterside patio, seating up to 100, and partially set about with flowers in tubs and boxes. Inside, as well as a friendly welcome from Derek, Alan and Rene and staff, you will find the lounge is paved with York stone, the ceiling beamed, an inglenook fireplace and fine brasses. The menus are enormous, but prices are not! No surprise, then, that this is a very popular establishment, and the 28 seater restaurant is often full, so do book if possible. Good atmosphere, and children welcome. Large car park.

THE WHITE LION

High Street, Hampton-in-Arden.   Tel. (0675) 442833
>   Location: Village centre, on B4102.
>   Credit cards: Access, Visa.
>   Accommodation: 3 doubles.
>   Bitters: Traditional Bass, Brew XI, Highgate Mild.
>   Lagers: Carling.

Examples of bar meals (lunch & evening, Mon. – Sat., plus Trad. Sun. lunch): *homemade steak & kidney pie, chilli, curry, cottage pie, lasagne, steaks, mixed grill, gammon, chicken, scampi, cod, omelettes, salads, vegetarian choices.*
Examples of restaurant meals (evenings only, Mon. – Sat.): *various steaks, mixed grill, breast fillet of chicken on chasseur sauce, Lynn's old fashioned steak & kidney pie, trout, vegetarian choices.*

At 600 years, this former farmhouse could be said to be ancient, but the church opposite is by far the senior, and is mentioned in Domesday. The inn is constructed, not unusually for that time, from solid oak ship's timbers, but in this case they were 'coming home', as this is where the oaks were grown in the first place. Being so steeped in history, one would expect a tradional English country inn at its best, and one would not be disappointed. The local cricket team and bellringers gather here, but there are no 'cliques', and strangers meet with a warm welcome. John and Linda Moffitt are the custodians, and present good food and beer in the bars and dining room, and allow children. Though not far from Birmingham, its airport and the N.E.C., this is a pleasant country area in which to stay. Large car park. CAMRA pub of the year for the Solihull area.

THE BULL INN

Weston-under-Wetherley, Leamington Spa.   Tel. (0926) 632392

       Location: Edge of village on B4453.
    Credit cards: Not accepted.
        Bitters: Marstons Pedigree, Burton Bitter, Mercian mild. Guinness.
        Lagers: Stella Artois, Heineken, Swan Light.

Examples of bar meals (lunch & evening, Mon. – Sat. Trad. Sun. lunch. No food Sun. evening): *mushrooms in breadcrumbs deepfried & served with garlic or blue cheese dip, peach halves stuffed with prawns & tuna, pan fried pork, lemon chicken, duck in orange sauce, salmon, honey baked ham with peaches, steaks, seafood platter, spicy broccoli au gratin, vegetable lasagne. Homemade sherry trifle, treacle tart, apple pie, chocolate fudge cake, special icecream menu. Daily lunchtime specials.*

The village pub occupies a special place in English affections, and here is a fine example of why this is so. The locals' bar is well frequented, but the welcome is as genuine and the food as good if you are just passing through. Pat and Maurice Jones have earned a reputation for homecooked fare; the menu is varied and comprehensive, and supplemented by interesting daily specials. A range of liqueur coffees is a pleasant way to round off the meal. Although dining is informal, one is invited to ring ahead if possible to reserve a table. Children are welcome if eating with adults, or take them into the garden. An easy pub to find, and not one to be missed. Car park.

THE OLD SMITHY

Green Lane, Church Lawford, nr Rugby.   Tel. (0203) 542333

       Location: Village centre, just off A428.
  Credit cards: Access, Visa.
        Bitters: Shipstons, Ansells, Tetley.
        Lagers: Lowenbrau, Castlemaine, Skol.

Examples of bar meals (lunch & evening, except Sun. evening): *tagliatelle Bolognese with hot fresh bread, Angus steaks, chicken ham & veg. pie, platter of potato skins with 4 different fillings, California beefburger, salmon steaks in cream & wine sauce, trout, scampi, vegetable curry, daily specials. Hot cherry pie, creme caramel, Old Smithy speciality icecreams. Trad. Sun. roasts.*

John and Kathy O'Neill arrived only in December '91, but have been quick to make their mark with their sociability and a varied menu of wholesome, homecooked food. They have acquired a good village pub, steeped in tradition: the bar is part of the original building which, incredibly, dates from the 13th century, and always features in local histories. Oak is much in evidence, and the timbers support an exceptionally good brass collection. A log fire sheds its inimitable warmth. Chance your arm on the skittle alley, or perhaps you may prefer pool, darts or dominoes in the Public bar. Children may play in the garden, but are also permitted inside. Those with a taste for the macabre should visit nearby Kings Newnham church, known for its mysterious coffins! Ample parking.

THE HARVESTER

Church Road, Long Itchington, nr Rugby.   Tel. (0926) 812698
      Location: Village centre, ¹/₄ mile off A423.
  Credit cards: Visa, Mastercard.
      Bitters: Hook Norton, Old Hooky, weekly guest.
      Lagers: Carlsberg, Carlsberg Export.

Examples of bar meals (lunch & evening, 7 days): *homemade soup, chilli, mixed grill, lasagne, faggots, pork curry, cottage pie, chicken Florentine, scampi, plaice, pizza, homecooked ham/beef, ploughman's, toasted sandwiches.*
Examples of restaurant meals (as above, except Sun evenings): *steaks, grilled trout with prawns, pork scallopi a la marsala, lamb chops bar-man, chicken Kiev, fillet steak Rossini. Trad. Sun. roasts.*

400 yards off the A423, next to the parish church and square in the traditional heart of the village, you will find The Harvester. A freehouse with a well deserved reputation for its quality beers and food, and its warm welcome to families, it has been recommended by the CAMRA Good Beer guide every year since 1985, and by the Coventry Evening Telegraph Good Pub Food Guide. The charming restaurant is well patronised by visitors and locals alike. Both pub and restaurant are well used by local societies, Young Farmers, Women's Institute, Round Table and Parish Council.

THE SHOULDER OF MUTTON

Sawbridge Road, Grandborough, nr Rugby.   Tel. (0788) 810306

Location:	Village centre, 2 miles off A45 near Dunchurch.
Credit cards:	Visa, Mastercard.
Bitters:	Wadworth 6X, Flowers, Marston's Pedigree.
Lagers:	Stella Artois, Heineken.

Examples of bar meals (lunch & evening, except Sun. evening): *seafood tortellini, ham & cheese pancakes, scampi, chicken filled with cheese & mushrooms, lemon sole filled with crab meat, gammon, curry, lasagne, steaks, tikka-filled jacket potatoes, ploughman's, toasties.*

A few of the many regulars here may prefer you to drive past on the A45, because they want to keep their favourite village local to themselves! In truth, the atmosphere is a very friendly one, and Paul and Anne Kambanis, licensees since summer '91, are genuinely pleased to greet allcomers. The lounge is snug and cosy, just the place to relax after a long ramble in the beautiful countryside in these parts. The public bar, with skittles, pool, dominoes and darts is always bright and lively, and teams participate in local leagues. Further amusement, in the shape of petanque, is to be had in the large garden, which has plenty of seating and a play area for children. Add to all this good ale and food, and you have the best kind of country inn, true to its origins, and without the instant ageing of the plastic designer pub of which we all know and dread.

THE OLD MINT

Coventry Street, Southam.   Tel. (0926) 812339

Location: Town centre, opp. police station, on A423.
Credit cards: Not accepted.
Bitters: Wadworth 6X, Marstons Pedigree, Taylor's Landlord, Hook Norton, Flowers Original, Boddingtons, Bass, monthly guest. Bateman's Mild.
Lagers: Stella Artois, Heineken.

Examples of bar meals (lunch & evening, 7 days): *steak & kidney pudding, cottage pie, lasagne, gammon, scampi, plaice, minute steak, big steak specials, traditional sausages, Grandma Batty's Yorkshire puddings, salads, jacket potatoes, sandwiches, ploughman's.*
Examples of restaurant meals (as above): *prawn Italienne, steaks, chicken cordon bleu, vegetarian dishes. Homemade apple pie, bread & butter pudding, sticky toffee pudding, treacle sponge, spotted dick.*

This superb 14th century building became briefly the royal mint (hence the name) back in 1642, when King Charles I melted down local silver here to pay his army. The sense of history is inescapable, it seeps out of every half-timbered wall, oak beam and open log fire, reinforced by a collection of guns and swords in the Armoury Bar. Here you will also find one of the best selection of good ales in the county, meriting praise from CAMRA guides. The cosy Buttery Bar, tiny but full of atmosphere, serves as the restaurant. Children are welcome, and will love the ornamental fish pond with fountain, and the bouncing castle in the garden. Geoff and Sylvia Wright came here two years ago, and have made significant improvements, revised the menus, and plan to add accommodation – Stratford, Warwick, Banbury and Coventry are not far.

Warwickshire

THE GRANVILLE ARMS

52 Wellesbourne Road, Barford.   Tel: (0926) 624236
        Location: Village centre, on A429
    Credit cards: Access, Visa
          Bitters: Flowers IPA, Everards Beacon, Boddington, Bass, Brains dark
                    mild.
          Lagers: Stella Artois, Heineken.

Examples of bar/restaurant meals (lunch & evening, 7 days): *chilli chicken, casserole of beef & red wine, gamekeeper's pie, steaks, Highland beef, garlic cream chicken, homecooked meats and quiches, creamed fishermans's pie, goujons of salmon, special evening fish dish, self-serve salads, vegetarian dishes, doorstep sandwiches, daily specials, Trad. Sun. lunches.*

One of only two survivors of 12 pubs in the village, The Granville has long been the hub of local life, a place to meet and exchange friendly banter. Yet there is no hint of cliques – strangers are made especially welocme. Proprietors Tom and Gill Douglas were themselves strangers eight years ago (Tom from Belfast, Gill from Yorkshire). Their early 19th century pub lends itself to easy relaxation: cosy and full of character, warmed by open fires. Food (homecooked) enjoys an excellent reputation for quality, and prices are modest. Look out for special theme evenings (Caribbean, for example), held in the new restaurant (available for private functions). Children are welcome, and there's a play area in the large garden, which also has a patio and barbecue. Darts, dominoes and crib. Car park. Warwick Castle only five minutes, Stratford just 10.

THE HOLLY BUSH INN

Bush Lane, Priors Marston, nr Rugby.   Tel. (0327) 60934

Location:	Village centre, near church.
Credit cards:	Visa, Mastercard, Eurocard.
Bitters:	Hook Norton, Marston's Pedigree, guests.
Lagers:	Stella Artois, Heineken.

Examples of bar meals (lunch & evening, 7 days): *beef & Guinness pie, steak, roast chicken, lasagne, vegetarian dishes, daily specials.*

Examples of restaurant meals (every evening, plus trad. Sun. lunch)*: Holly Bush terrine, garlic mushrooms, sirloin & fillet steaks in sauces, duck with pear & Madeira sauce, lamb with honey & mead, trout, plaice, vegetarian selection.*

NB Pub open from 12 to 3pm Mon – Thurs and Sunday, 12 to 4pm Fri & Sat, 6 to 11pm Mon – Sat, 7 to 10:30pm Sun.

Originally the village bakehouse, locals would come in for a loaf of bread as well as a jug of ale. An old oven was uncovered recently during extension work to create a new restaurant, where the tradition of serving good ale and food is still observed, only far more diverse and interesting than could have been envisaged in the 17th century. Set deep in the Warwickshire countryside, it's a characterful stone building, full of exposed timbers, with two large fireplaces in the bar and one in the dining room – a most agreeable environment in which to partake of excellent fare. Hospitable hosts are Steve and Liz Newby, who welcome children and have a games room and a play area in the large garden. Good parking.

THE ANTELOPE INN

Lighthorne, nr Warwick.   Tel. (0926) 651295

     Location: Village centre, off B4100 (A41), 8 miles south of Warwick.
  Credit cards: Access, Visa.
      Bitters: Flowers Original, IPA, Boddington, Wadworth 6X.
      Lagers: Stella Artois, Heineken.

Examples of bar/restaurant meals (lunch & evening, 7 days): *Japanese style king prawns with garlic dip, 7-piece mixed grill, homemade steak & kidney pie, steaks, homecooked ham/beef, trout, salmon, vegtarian dishes, daily specials.*

The Antelope has matured quietly here in this pleasant village for 350 years. It is particularly worth a visit on a sunny day, for the banked garden (with tables and chairs) is a delight, enhanced by the restful sounds of a little splashing waterfall. Brian and Pat Jones are the fortunate proprietors, and they will be pleased to welcome you and any children with friendly service and good, wholesome food at very fair prices. The restaurant decor celebrates the theme of a somewhat less friendly era, that of Cromwell – breast plates, swords, guns and even a cannon are mounted on the walls! Yet this is a peaceful haven, away from the hustle and bustle, but less than a mile from the B4100 – just the spot to get life back in perspective! Large car park.

THE GAYDON INN

Banbury Road, Gaydon.   Tel. (0926) 640388

    Location: On B4100, $1/2$ mile from jncn 12 of M40.
Credit cards: Not accepted.
     Bitters: Brew XI, Bass Special.
      Lagers: Carling, Tennents, Tennents Extra.

Examples of bar meals (lunch & evening, 7 days. Breakfasts 8 – 11am): *homemade soup, chilli, steak & kidney pie, lasagne, chicken Kiev, homecooked ham off-the-bone (speciality), steaks, seafood, vegetarian dishes, daily specials. Trad. Sun. roasts.*

Said to be one of the oldest coaching inns in the country (16th century), many an unsavoury character has warmed himself by the open fires in the course of its long history. Most notorious were John Smith and his Culworth Gang, who relieved travellers of their purses and spent some of the proceeds here. Ask John and Joan Taylor behind the bar if you want to know more about the exploits of these and other rogues. It is not difficult to recapture the spirit of the past amongst the ancient timbers, despite modern improvements. Nowadays the atmosphere is rather friendlier and the food much superior, thanks to Joan's experience in home cooking, and may be taken in either bar or dining room. They welcome children, who will no doubt be fascinated by the rare sheep and poultry kept by John in a paddock visible from the garden.

THE CASTLE INN

Edgehill, nr Banbury. Tel. (0295) 87255
Location: 1 mile off A422.
Credit cards: Access, Visa.
Bitters: Hook Norton.
Lagers: Heineken, Carlsberg.

Examples of bar meals (lunch & evening, 7 days): *prawn cocktail, lasagne, steaks, mixed grill (speciality), seafood platter, homemade steak & kidney pie, gammon, plaice, vegetarian dish, ploughman's, sandwiches, daily specials.*

This extraordinary edifice would merit a visit even were it not also a good pub, so steeped in history is it. Built as a folly between 1747 and 1750, it stands on the spot where King Charles I raised his standard before the Battle of Edgehill, fought on October 23rd, 1642. Indeed, the garden commands a panorama of the battlefield itself, and the event is described by a picture hanging in the entrance. Civil War memorabilia fill one of the timbered bars, while the other celebrates the more peacable theme of agriculture with old farming implements. For more of the former, visit the Edgefield Museum at nearby Farnborough Hall (Upton House is also close). Custodians of this unique place are John and Gill Blann, very experienced in the trade, who serve good staple food, plus an outsanding range of traditional and fruit wines, and malt whiskies. Children welcome – play area in the garden. Pool and darts.

THE BELL INN

Alderminster, nr Stratford-on-Avon.   Tel. (0789) 450414

       Location: A34 3 miles south of Stratford.
Credit cards: Access, Visa.
         Bitters: Flowers.
         Lagers: Stella Artois, Heineken.

Examples from menu (lunch & evening, 7 days): *venison & pheasant pie, calves liver in cream with sage, garlic king prawns, fresh Scotch salmon, chicken supreme in tarragon sauce, lamb & almond casserole, rogan josh curry, creamy mushrooms on toast, hazelnut roast. Fresh fish a speciality. Fresh strawberry pavlova, hot chocolate fudge pudding, syrup & walnut tart. Quick 2-course business lunch Mon – Fri. Slimmers menu at all times.*

A novel and exciting approach to good food belies this outwardly traditional coaching inn. Keith and Vanessa Brewer enjoy running an occasional 'theme night', and sport the appropriate national costume – for example, Italian, French, Indian, Old English, with a wine list to match. One thing which doesn't change is the very high standard of presentation and quality which has earned The Bell such an enviable reputation. The blackboard menu changes daily, and fresh seafood is the forte. Children are welcome if accompanied, and non-smokers have an area set aside for them. Inside is tastefully furnished in pine, with sturdy rustic tables complemented by the ancient beams. Outside is a large secluded courtyard garden, and ample parking.

THE HORSESHOE INN

Church Street, Shipston-on-Stour   Tel. (0608) 61225

Location:	Town centre, on A34 10 miles south of Stratford.
Credit cards:	Access, Visa, Diners, Amex.
Accommodation:	4 doubles, with col. tv's, tea & coffee facilities.
Bitter:	Webster's Green Label, Ruddles. Ansell's Mild. Guinness.
Lagers:	Fosters, Carlsberg, Holsten.

Examples of bar meals (lunchtime only, 7 days): *scampi, plaice, roast chicken, salads, ploughman's, daily specials eg cottage pie, lasagne, steak & kidney pie, liver & onions.*
Examples of restaurant meals (lunch & evening, 7 days): *smoked salmon, rack of lamb, beef Wellington, game casserole, Aberdeen Angus steaks with variety of sauces (speciality), mixed grills, fisherman's platter, seafood Provencale, vegetarian dishes. Trad. Sun. roasts.*

This strikingly pretty black-and-white inn is the second oldest building in Shipston, and fortunately was not damaged by a major fire in the town 150 years ago. Wherever situated, it would be a lovely place to stay, but there is the additional bonus of being so well placed for Stratford, Warwick and the Cotswolds. Roger and Shirley came here late in 1989, and have brought to The Horseshoe personality and amicability. Their panelled restaurant has an outstanding menu; amongst the range of homecooked fare Aberdeen Angus steaks are a succulent speciality, but there are ample alternatives from which to choose. Children are welcome, and dogs if well-behaved, and to the rear is a very attractive walled garden with additional lawn (barbecues held from time to time). Large car park.

THE HOWARD ARMS

Lower Green, Ilmington, nr Shipston-on-Stour.　　　　Tel. (060 882) 226

Location:	Village centre, 8 miles from Stratford.
Credit cards:	Access, Visa, Amex.
Accommodation:	2 doubles, en suite, tea & coff.
Bitters:	Flowers, Marston's Pedigree, guests.
Lagers:	Stella Artois, Heineken.

Examples of bar meals (lunch & evening, 7 days): *steak & kidney pie, seafood croissant, crispy haddock, chicken curry, vegetarian dishes, ploughman's, blackboard specials. Children's menu.*
Examples of restaurant meals (evenings only Mon – Sat, plus Trad Sun lunch): *calf's sweetbreads, fillet steak with tarragon & butter sauce, supreme of salmon grilled with vermouth & chive butter. Pineapple spiced with black pepper & red wine, chocolate roulade.*

The name of Howard is an illustrious one: it was a Howard who commanded the navy against the Spanish Armada, and his kinsman died leading the vanguard at Bosworth. Another great name, Winston Churchill, took refuge here from the stress of war. Replete with timbers, flagstoned floors and Cotswold fireplaces, it is full of character, including the newly redecorated restaurant. New hands David and Melanie Smart and chef patron Alan Thompson share the premises with an old hand, ephemeral Charlie. Alan's skills in the kitchen have maintained a place in a major good pub guide, and extend to outside catering. New bedrooms mean one can stay to enjoy Hidcote Gardens, Camden Hill and the Cotswolds. Children welcome – play area in garden.

THE COLLEGE ARMS

Lower Quinton, Stratford-on-Avon.   Tel. (0789) 720342

Location: Village centre, off B4632.
Credit cards: Access, Visa.
Bitters: Flowers, guests.
Lagers: Stella Artois, Heineken.

photo P.A.Cruford, Stratford.

Examples of bar/restaurant meals (lunch & evening, 7 days): *homemade steak & kidney pie, curry, chilli, pasta dishes, gammon & eggs (renowned), vegetarian dishes, blackboard specials eg coronation chicken, sweet & sour pork, beef & Guinness, duck & orange, game. Trad. Sun. roasts. Selection of starters & sweets.*

Henry VIII granted the inn and surrounding land to Magdalen College, Oxford (which retained ownership until quite recently), and they bear the same coat of arms. His daughter, Elizabeth I, granted rare Royal Arms to the church, making this a very well connected village! With such a background, one would expect a pub of character, and one would not be disappointed. The lounge, in particular, is quite beguiling – exposed beams and stonework, and wood panelled snug with inglenook fireplace (to which there would seem to be one ephemeral gentleman who likes to turn his chair). There's also a public bar with games, and an upstairs restaurant which doubles as a function room and is also available for small private parties. Tony and Lynn Smith, proprietors for five years, offer a wide ranging menu, and three or four times a year hold special evenings – Bavarian is especially popular. Accompanied children are permitted, and there's an aviary on the terrace. Car parking.

THE FLEECE

The Cross, Bretforton, nr Evesham.   Tel. (0386) 831173
        Location: Village centre, 30 yards from church.
    Credit cards: Not accepted.
          Bitters: Hook Norton, Pig's Ear, Old Spot, Brew XI.
          Lagers: Heineken. Plus Weston's Scrumpy cider.

Examples of bar meals (lunch & evening, except Mon evening): *steak & kidney pie, steaks, Gloucester sausages, chilli, lasagne, homecured ham, scampi, plaice, ratatouille lasagne, ploughman's, sandwiches, daily specials. Apple pie, lemon meringue, gateau.*

Can it really be as exquisite as it looks? The answer is yes, for this 14th century farmhouse is considered rare enough to have been acquired by the National Trust, on the understanding that it would continue to be run as an unspoilt country pub. Its long history is described in a leaflet, but if you want to hear about the ghosts ask landlord Norman Griffiths, "if you have hours to spare and he's not too busy!" More tangible attractions are the Dugout (formerly a pantry), the Pewter Room housing the famous Fleece collection, and the Brewhouse, these last two having 'Witchmarks' to keep out evil spirits. But do find time to eat and drink! The Fleece is rated by both good pub and good beer guides, and connoisseurs of the latter should not miss the festival on 10th, 11th and 12th July 1992. Morris Dancing and brass bands are other regular diversions. Children welcome – garden has play area and barbecue. Darts. Barn available for functions.

THE QUEENS HOTEL

Queens Hill, Belbroughton, nr Stourbridge.   Tel. (0562) 730276

      Location: Village centre, next to brook.
Credit cards: Not accepted.
       Bitters: Marstons.
        Lagers: Stella Artois, Heineken.

Examples of bar meals (lunch & evening, except Sunday evening): *cheese ham & onion pie, lasagne, hot chilli, steak & kidney pie, scampi, steaks, salads, seasonal blackboard specials eg grouse, pheasant. Plum crumble, treacle tart, hot ginger cake.*
Examples of restaurant meals (for private parties only, by arrangement): *roast duck, roast beef, fresh salmon from Wye, lobster.*

The Vintage Bentley Owners Club meets here regularly (as the photo suggests), and their good taste obviously extends beyond classic cars! The name is misleading, for it is not actually an hotel, but it is a pub well above the norm, and of considerable character. Belbroughton is one of the prettier villages in these parts, and 19th century 'Queens' stands right at its heart, the large car park bordered by a stream. New owners John and Dianne Narbett, who for 13 years were landlords of The Bell just a mile down the road, firmly intend to retain the homely atmosphere, free of gaming machines and juke box, and to serve homecooked traditional English cuisine. An upstairs dining room is reserved for private parties, and on Christmas Eve there's a special party for children, to which Santa Claus always drops in.

THE EAGLE & SUN

Hanbury Wharf, Hanbury Road, Droitwich.   Tel. (0905) 770130

Location: B4090 1½ miles from Droitwich on Stratford road.
Credit cards: Not accepted.
Bitters: M & B, Bass, Springfield, Brew XI, M & B Mild.
Lagers: Carling, Tennents Extra. Draught ciders, low alcohol ales.

Examples of bar meals (lunchtime 7 days, evenings except Sundays): *various steaks, gammon, chicken boursin, chicken curry madras, rainbow trout, swordfish steak, mixed grill, homemade steak & kidney pie, vegetarian lasagne, omelettes, ploughman's, daily blackboard specials.*

The Worcester-Birmingham canal runs by the attractive gardens, and dining at the water's edge is a very pleasant experience. This is a spot much favoured by boating people, for there's a marina opposite with overnight moorings. But the welcome is equally warm to locals and visitors alike, from Sandra and David Mayne, who have built this into a lively and bustling pub, noted for excellent home prepared food in very generous helpings. No surprise, then, that table reservations are advisable at weekends. A separate room with bar and seating for 30 is ideal for a private party, and coach parties are readily accommodated with advance notice. Children are welcome at lunchtimes. Local historians note that it was built in 1835, and was part of the Hadzor Estate.

THE ROCK TAVERN

Wilden Lane, Stourport-on-Severn.   Tel. (0299) 822962

Location: Mid-way between Kidderminster and Stourport.
Credit cards: Access, Visa, Diners, Amex.
Bitters: Holts, Tetley, guest.
Lagers: Skol, Lowenbrau. Plus Murphy's, Guinness, cider.

Examples of bar meals (lunch & evening, 7 days): *steaks, chicken chasseur, gammon, plaice, salads, sandwiches, vegetarian by request, daily specials.*
Examples of restaurant meals (as above): *fillet of beef teryaki, half crispy roast duck, Caribbean pork, fresh fish of the day, steaks, vegetable bake, daily specials. Trad. Sun. roasts.*
NB Pub open daily 11am to 11pm.

One of the best known pubs in these parts, The Rock deserves its excellent reputation for good, home prepared food. There's usually a choice of five fresh vegetables, and portions are not niggardly. Business people can even fax their menu so that it is ready on arrival – modern technology put to best possible use! In every other respect this is a traditional cottage style pub, 18th century, full of atmosphere and overlooking the River Stour. Original paintings adorn the rustic brickwork and beams in both bars and upstairs 'barn style' restaurant. Legend has it that sandstone caves to the rear once led to Hartlebury Castle, and other local attractions include Severn Valley Railway, Safari Park, Leapgate Country Park and the picturesque town of Stourport a mile away. Owners (for eight years) John Armstrong and Jean Wilson run the bars and restaurant, while Jean's son Kevin is the chef.

THE DOG AT DUNLEY

Dunley, nr Stourport-on-Severn.   Tel. (0299) 822833
          Location: On A451 Stourport to Gt Witley road.
      Credit cards: Access, Visa.
   Accommodation: 1 single, 2 doubles (en suite), 2 twins. From £15 pp.
           Bitters: Holts, Burtons, Tetley.
           Lagers: Lowenbrau, Castlemaine.

Examples of bar/dining room meals (lunch & evening, 7 days): *garlic mushrooms, steak & kidney pie in Guinness, steaks, mixed grill (noted), curry, lasagne, hot chilli, cottage pie, mariner's delight, prawn Portuguese, salmon, trout, cheese & leek bake, cheese & broccoli bake, daily specials. Homemade desserts. Trad. Sun. roasts £5.95.*

The wisteria makes a stunning display when in full bloom – it may be as old as the building (1610), and has the rare distinction of a preservation order. But there are other, better reasons for a visit to this delightful, cottagey inn. The food, a blend of traditional English and continental, is all homecooked and excellent value. The atmosphere is as warm and cheering (assisted by coal fires in winter) as one would hope for in a true village local, hosted by new licensees Simon Haynes and Penny Neaverson. Families are always welcome, and the very pleasant garden has bowling green, play area and barbecue. Indoor entertainment is in the form of darts, pool and a piano, and there is an annexe for private parties and meetings. Being in pleasant countryside and handy for many attractions, The Dog makes a marvellous base for an extended stay.

THE COLLIERS ARMS

Tenbury Road, Clows Top, nr Kidderminster.   Tel. (029 922) 242

Location:	A456 between Tenbury Wells and Bewdley.
Credit cards:	Access, Visa, Switch.
Accommodation:	Hotel block and conference centre planned.
Bitters:	Ansells.
Lagers:	Lowenbrau.

Examples of bar/restaurant meals (lunch & evening, 7 days): *beef provencale, pork steak in whole grain mustard & cream sauce, chicken marsala, half roast duck, breast of chicken stuffed with garlic butter & mushrooms, steak & kidney pie, fresh fish dishes, lasagne, chilli, spicy broccoli au gratin, cheese & nut croquets, courgette & mushroom lasagne. Large variety of sweets. Children's menu.*

"The House for Good Food" – no idle boast, for over the past few years (under the personal supervision of the Sankey family), this 19th century pub has established a first rate reputation for excellent cooking (Wyre Forest award winner for food and hygiene), as well as good value. It is thus very popular with the locals, but even when busy the staff are friendly and helpful, the service prompt. No gaming machines intrude on the conversational ambience. Open log fires radiate their inimitable warm glow over the comfortable, homely bars in winter, but in summer many choose to dine al fresco in the very pretty garden with patio and tables. There used to be a number of small coal mines around here (hence the name), but it has all reverted to farmland, and the countryside is very pretty. Children welcome. Facilities for disabled.

THE RED LION INN

Stifford's Bridge, nr Malvern.   Tel. (0886) 880318

Location:	A4103 Hereford to Worcester road.
Credit cards:	Access, Visa.
Accommodation:	1 twin (£35, £20 single), 1 family (£43.75). Tv's, tea & coff. Luxury bathroom has exercise bike!
Bitters:	Banks, Ansells, Woods, Knights.
Lagers:	Grolsch, Harp, Kronenbourg.

Examples of bar meals (lunch & evening, 7 days, but Sun. evening April – Oct. only): *smoked mackerel pate, whitebait, homemade pies, liver & bacon casserole, lamb or chicken curry, lasagne (vegetarian option), spinach cheese & mushroom pancakes, chilli, steaks, ham & beef platter, salads, ploughman's. Children's menu.*

Examples of restaurant meals (evenings Wed – Sat, trad. Sun. lunch): *noisettes of lamb with redcurrant & burgundy sauce, medallions of pork, poached salmon with white wine sauce, poached breast of chicken stuffed with asparagus & wrapped in puff pastry, sirloin steak, chef's specials.*

Now with new accommodation, this charming beamed freehouse is ideally placed as a roadside stop for families touring the Malverns – Elgar country. The large garden, at its best in summertime, abounds with colourful floral displays. Children will love the play area, whilst parents unwind on the attractive patio – the atmosphere is restful and friendly, with careful volume control of background music. In inclement weather the log fires extend their incomparable welcome. But it is probably for the excellence and value of homecooked food that the inn is best known – Proprietors Rachel and Andrew Williams belong to both the Guild of Master Caterers and Guild of Master Cellarmen. The restaurant is well suited to private parties, weddings etc. Easy parking.

THE ANCHOR INN & RESTAURANT

Drakes Street, Welland, Malvern.   Tel. (0684)592317

Location:	A4104, Upton-on-Severn to Malvern road.
Credit cards:	Access, Visa, Eurocard, Mastercard.
Bitters:	Marstons Pedigree, Flowers S.P.A., Swan Light. Murphy's.
Lagers:	Stella Artois, Heineken. Plus Scrumpy Jack cider.

Examples of bar meals (lunch & evening, 7 days): *homemade soup, grilled gammon steak, deep fried scampi, steaks, fillet of plaice with prawn stuffing, poached salmon trout, variety of salads, ploughman's, vegetable gratin, aubergine & mushroom lasagne, chef's specials.*

Examples of restaurant meals (evenings only, Tues. – Sat.): *homemade parsnip & apple soup, spiced prawn pilaff; whole baby sole pan-fried with banana liqueur, steak au poivre, breast of chicken with marjoram & cucumber. Hazelnot pavlova with fresh fruit, hot fudge bananas, apple mint souffle. Chef's specials. Children's menu.*

"Let the guest be entertained here. Our life is simple. What we cannot afford we do not offer, but what good cheer we can give, we give gladly." So declare Pauline and John Elbro on the menu; a simple philosophy, but one which few would refute. Their very comely black-and-white cottage pub, dating from the 1600's, was established as a pub by an ex sea captain (hence the name) and, with an obvious eye for design, has a pleasing combination inside of pink walls, old beams, inglenooks, and stylish chintz furnishing. There are no steps anywhere – good news for the disabled – and the garden has a patio with tables and chairs and children's play area. Food, whether in the bar or restaurant, is highly creative, with separate sections for vegetarians and children. With new accommodation, one will be able to dwell longer, and enjoy the lovely countryside of The Malverns.

THE THREE KINGS INN

Hanley Castle, nr Upton-upon-Severn   Tel. (0684) 592686

Location:	Village centre.
Credit cards:	Not accepted.
Accommodation:	1 twin, (£25 sngl, £40 dbl). Private bath, tea & coffee.
Bitters:	Thwaites, Butcombe, Jolly Roger, Bass, guest.
Lagers:	Carlsberg, Tennents Extra.

Examples of bar meals (lunch & evening, except Sun evening): *chicken en croute with mushrooms & soft cheese, beef Wellington, steaks, pork chop, salmon en croute with broccoli & cream sauce, plaice stuffed with prawns & mushrooms, trout, scampi, omelettes, ploughman's, sandwiches. Blackberry & apple pancake rolls & cream, chocolate trufito, Belgian chocolate icecream.*

Incredibly, this unspoilt 15th century inn has been run by the same family for 80 years, currently by landlady Sheila Roberts, who's been here for the last 30. It is encouraging to know that such rooted family commitments persist in an age of "fun pubs" run by indifferent young managers. It is reputed to have been a salt-bartering centre in the Middle Ages, and is one of only four pubs so named in the country. All the trappings of antiquity are there: exposed timbers and brickwork, inglenooks, quarry tile flooring, copper and brass, old domestic and agricultural implements. A jukebox is strictly taboo, but there is live entertainment Sunday evenings and a folk club alternate Thursdays. Darts, crib, shove ha'penny and dominoes provide quiet amusement. A room is set aside for families, and another is suitable for private parties. Paved front courtyard. Easy parking. Recommended by national good pub guides.

THE TALBOT HOTEL

Knightwick, nr Worcester.   Tel. (0886) 21235

Location:	Just off A44 near junction with B4197.
Credit cards:	Access, Visa.
Accommodation:	10 bedrooms (7 en suite).
Bitters:	Flowers IPA, Bass, Banks, Castle Eden.
Lagers:	Tennents Pils & Extra, Low Alcohol.

Examples of bar/restaurant meals (lunch & evening, 7 days. Limited menu Sunday evenings): *sirloin steak, lamb noisettes with fresh ginger & yoghurt sauce, pork loin & green peppercorn sauce, halibut steak, whole lemon sole, chicken breast with sherry & spring onion sauce, pheasant marinated in fresh ginger & pineapple, steak & kidney pie, vegetarian dishes, chef's specials.*

If you are the sporty type but shy away from stark modern sports clubs, you will be delighted by The Talbot, run by the Clifts, brother and sister. Their 14th century inn maintains a firm grip on the traditional, with a mass of oak beams, log fires, and walls hung with unusual hunting prints and paintings. One may relax with some excellent food (cooked to order) in either bar or restaurant, but there's a wealth of activities to pursue: squash, sauna and solarium, clay pigeon shooting in summer, pheasant shooting in winter (please pre-book), and horse riding. The Worcestershire Way walk passes through here, and there's also good fishing on the nearby river Teme. Large garden. Children welcome.

THE WHITE HORSE INN

The Square, Clun.   Tel. Clun (058 84) 305

Location:	Town centre, on B4368
Credit cards:	Not accepted.
Accommodation:	1 single, 1 twin, 1 family. £16.95 pp.
Bitters:	Draught Bass, Draught Worthington.
Lagers:	Carling, Tennents.

Examples of bar meals (lunch & evening, 7 days): *homemade soup, chilli, curries, ham & eggs, plaice, seafood platter, bean hotpot, pasta with mushrooms & tomato sauce, ploughman's, sandwiches. Apple pie, fruit flans.*

In a designated Area of Outstanding Natural Beauty not far from the Welsh border, this part of Shropshire is blessed with some of the loveliest countryside in the region, delightful for walking. Having so stimulated an appetite, one would be well advised to repair to this attractive 18th century coaching inn in the village square. Warm and inviting, it is run entirely by owners Bruce and Christine, who came here four years ago. They present staple homecooked bar meals, supplemented by a vegetarian menu, and have been nominated for the next CAMRA guide. The single bar is agreeably traditional, with exposed beams and brickwork, stone fireplace, collection of farming tools and a small beer sign collection. Pool, darts and dominoes provide amusement. Children are welcome, and there is a garden. Parking in square.

THE SUN INN

Corfton, nr Craven Arms.   Tel. (0584) 73239
Location: B4368 7 miles from Ludlow.
Credit cards: Access, Visa.
Bitters: Bass, 2 or 3 guests. Murphy's stout.
Lagers: Heineken.

Examples of bar/restaurant meals (lunch & evening, 7 days): *homemade soup, oriental dimsoms, special mixed grill, steaks, duck a l'orange, chicken tikka, lasagne verdi, trout, plaice, scampi, filled jacket potatoes, vegetarian dishes, daily specials. Children's menu. Trad. Sun. roasts (booking advisd).*

The extraordinary tale of Mary Jones, born here as the daughter of a helper at the inn, deported more than once to Australia, and a colourful legend in her own lifetime, makes interesting reading – ask about it at the bar. Licensed in 1770, this friendly freehouse is the oldest licensed in beautiful Corvedale. Beneath the wealth of exposed beams is a lounge bar with dining area, where is served homecooked meals and snacks, and afternoon teas (children are especially welcome and have their own menu); also a large public bar (with eating area), with darts, pool and other games. Look for the old well in an extension to the dining room. In kind weather, many prefer to eat on the patio, and youngsters appreciate the garden with ducks and chickens, and an old tractor. The Pearce family extend a personal welcome to all, including hikers and ramblers, and are pleased to cater for coaches and parties up to 50.

THE PLOUGH INN

Claverley, Bridgnorth.　　　　　　　　　　　　　Tel. (074 66) 365

   Location: Village centre, one mile off A454.
  Credit cards: Access, Visa.
    Bitters: Burtons, all Ansells, guests.
    Lagers: Skol, Castlemaine, Lowenbrau.

Examples of bar meals (lunch & evening, Tues – Sat): *oriental chicken with sweet & sour sauce, beef & Guinness pie, lasagne, chilli, steaks, gammon, smoked trout, scampi, speciality dishes of the day (incl. vegetarian), salads, ploughman's, sandwiches. Homemade sweets.*
Examples of restaurant meals (as above, plus trad. Sun. lunch): *Mexican vol au vents, plaice paupiettes, selection of steaks, chicken Rossini, medallions of pork, beef & pepper casserole, trout with garlic & prawns. Pavlovas, cherry mille feuille, bread & butter pudding.*

Homecooked food and friendly staff and management are reason enough to make this a very popular pub locally, but it also happens to be a 400-year-old grade II black and white timbered building, in a delightful village in this conservation area – a photographer's dream when the gardens are full of flowers. A homely, comfortable atmosphere prevails inside; a large open brick fire casts a warm glow in winter over the many brasses mounted on the old beams; the good size lounge has a number of snug areas, and an interesting collection of coins may be seen across the top of the bar. David O'Gorman was the area manager for a brewery, but 'crossed the counter' about nine years ago, and knows how to please customers, serving wholesome and imaginative food accompanied by a good wine list. Children have their own room, and a play area in the large garden and patio (barbecues held). Close to Worfield Cactus Gardens and Severn Valley Railway. Parking for 200, easily accessible for disabled. Weddings and other functions catered for.

WENLOCK EDGE INN

Hilltop, Wenlock Edge. Tel. (074 636) 403

Location:	B4371, Much Wenlock to Church Stretton road.
Credit cards:	Not accepted.
Accommodation:	1 double, 4 twins, all en suite.
Bitters:	Burton, Wem, guests.
Lagers:	Carlsberg. Stowford Press cider.

Examples of bar/restaurant meals (lunch & evening, Tues. – Sun.): *homemade soup, steak & mushroom pie, prawn salad, honey baked ham, porkie pie, wedgie pie (venison & beef), apricot chicken, poached salmon, half duckling with cherry sauce, rump steak (evenings only). Hot chocolate fudge pudding (very popular), chocolate chimney, Bakewell tart, tipsy banana. Daily specials.*

Incredibly, the Edge is a 400 million years old coral reef, and this is the only pub on it, affording dramatic views and exhilirating walks. By comparison, the 300-year history of the inn is a mere twinkle, but long enough to accumulate a bounty of ghost stories, which Stephen Waring will be glad to recount. He and family of Harry, Joan and Diane like to keep conversation flowing, facilitated by the merciful absence of loud gaming machines or music. They will not only tell you about the past, but your own future, according to Chinese horoscopes! Originally quarrymen's cottages, the building is inevitably of lovely Wenlock stone. A cosy dining room (children welcome) is set aside for non-smokers (or eat on the patio), to better savour the excellent and most original home fare (rated by major guides), accompanied by a descriptive wine list. Large garden and car park. Ironbridge is within easy reach.

THE COALBROOKDALE INN

12 Wellington Road, Coalbrookdale.   Tel. (0952) 433953
         Location: 1/2 mile from Ironbridge.
      Credit cards: Not accepted.
    Accommodation: 1 double, 1 twin, 1 family. £15 pp incl.
           Bitters: 6 everchanging guests.
            Lagers: Becks, Carling, Tennents.

Examples of bar/dining room meals (12 – 2pm, 6 – 8pm Mon – Fri, plus Sat lunch): *blackboard menu, always changing – fresh seafood platter, Beamish bake pie, hot & spicy stir fry, luxurious filled baguettes & pitta breads. All prepared on the day. No French fries in the evenings.*

Known throughout the county for its fine ales, now acknowledged by CAMRA, this fine example of a Georgian house (1750) is within easy reach of one of the regions most important attractions: Ironbridge Gorge with its Iron Museum. The inn has its own absorbing collection of pump badges, ceramic and metallic. Well before the Industrial Revolution a witch was burned near here, and her ghost is said to walk, along with that of a marching soldier, perhaps. Mike (chef) and Corinne are attentive hosts, who take pride in serving 'real' food as well as ales. Menus change daily, and occasional special evenings add yet further variety. An area is set aside for children, and there's also a patio with barbecue. Darts. Car park.

Shrewsbury

THE CORNHOUSE RESTAURANT & WINE BAR

59a Wylecop, Shrewsbury.   Tel. (0743) 231991

Location:	Town centre.
Credit cards:	Access, Visa, Amex.
Bitters:	Everchanging guests.

Examples of bar/restaurant meals (lunch & evening, 7 days): *savoury vegetable pancakes with cheese sauce, spicy marinated chicken wings, prawns in lemon yoghurt & herbs (in filo pastry case), tenderloin of pork in mustard sauce, beef Guinness & oyster pie, chargrilled steaks, supreme of chicken with mango sauce, monkfish provencale on tagliatelle, trout with prawn & cream sauce, chargrilled duck breast with tropical fruit sauce, vegetable curry, daily specials.*

It's not an inn or pub, strictly speaking, but nevertheless well worth an inclusion on the strength of the good, fresh food prepared on the premises. And what absorbing premises they are: built in 1780 as a corn warehouse, many of the original features have been retained, like open fires, exposed timbers and brickwork. A wrought iron spiral staircase connects the three floors: on the ground floor is the wine bar which houses an everchanging art exhibition, on the first the restaurant, on the second a function room. Shrewsbury is one of our most historic and picturesque towns, and being so central The Cornhouse makes an excellent watering hole during a day's sightseeing. Children welcome. Live music Sundays. Ample parking nearby. Rated by Michelin and Egon Ronay.

THE RED LION

Longden Common, nr Shrewsbury.   Tel. (0743) 738889

Location:	Village centre, 5 miles off A5.
Credit cards:	Not accepted.
Accommodation:	1 single, 1 twin, 1 family, all en suite.
Bitters:	Burtonwood, James Forshaw.
Lagers:	Labatts, Lowenbrau, Fosters.

Examples of bar/restaurant meals (lunch & evening, 7 days): *homemade steak & onion pie, Lion grill, steaks (incl. 16oz T-bone), roast chicken, lasagne, mussels provencale, scampi, plaice, vegetarian dishes, omelettes, ploughman's, sandwiches, daily specials. Children's menu. Trad. Sun. roasts.*

Coalminers once thronged here, seeking rest and recreation after a hard day down the pits. That was a long time ago; coal mines are fast becoming just a memory, but the warm and friendly country pub, of which The Red Lion is a fine example, is still, happily, very much with us. Two fireplaces broadcast their inimitable glow over the timbers and brickwork, but in summer it is the barbecue which is lit in the garden, which also has a play area (children welcome inside, too). Darts and dominoes provide amusement, but licensees Hazel and Gordon also lay on special evenings and live entertainment. Mention must be made of the amazingly good value food – at £6.95, the T-bone is the most expensive item on the menu. The historic county town of Shrewsbury is nearby, as are Longmynd and Stiperstones; having comfortable bedrooms, The Red Lion is a useful base.

THE PLUME OF FEATHERS

Harley, nr Much Wenlock.   Tel. (0952) 727360
Location: On A458, 1¹/₂ miles Shrewsbury side of Much Wenlock.
Accommodation: 1 twin, 2 family (for 4 & 6), all en suite.
Bitters: John Smiths, Courage Directors, traditional guests.
Lagers: Fosters, Kronenbourg.

Examples of bar/restaurant meals (lunch & evening, 7 days): *starters: crown of melon with grapes & wild strawberry sorbet, garlic mushroom pancake in white wine sauce. Main: Feathers special mixed grill, homemade pies (eg rabbit, steak & kidney, vegetarian), salmon steak in prawn sauce, duck a l'orange, vegetarian (eg vol au vents with herb mushroom & onion filling, vegetable lasagne. Sweets: homemade fruit pie, homemade gateaux, speciality icecream dishes.*
NB Restaurant 50 covers, booking advised weekends.

Sitting below the impressive Wenlock Edge Woods, The Plume of Feathers dates from around 1620, and its solid exposed timbers and two-feet-thick stone walls suggest it was built to last. The lounge bar is distinguished by the Charles I carved oak bar back, inglenook fireplaces and a full suit of armour! Families are welcome, and a large play area and beer garden is located to the rear. Hosts Peter and Beryl Hitchin subscribe to the policy that personal recommendation of their good food and traditional ales is sufficient to fill the restaurant most weekends. An ideal base for Ironbridge Gorge, Much Wenlock, Shrewsbury and Bridgnorth.

THE NEW INN

Hook-a-Gate, nr Shrewsbury.   Tel. (0743) 860223

       Location: 3 miles south of Shrewsbury on Longden road.
Credit cards: Not accepted.
        Bitters: Bass, guest.
        Lagers: Carling, Tennents.

Examples of bar meals (lunch & evening, 7 days): *homemade beef in beer pie, chilli, lasagne, chicken breast, plaice, ploughman's, sandwiches (lunch only), daily specials. Children's menu.*

Examples of restaurant meals (as above): *seafood au gratin, New Inn mixed grill, steaks, duck a l'orange, chicken & mushroom pie, curry, rainbow trout with prawns, darne of Greenland salmon, plaice stuffed with prawns & mushrooms, lemon sole. Trad. Sun. roasts.*

Somewhat a misnomer, The New Inn is actually about 250 years old, and for about one third of that time has been in the hands of the Hunter family. Rod Hunter, latest in the line, recalls that his grandmother used to brew her own beer, and supplied milk to the village from her smallholding. He also says he has heard mysterious footsteps on several occasions at 10:20am! Unspoilt by the ravages of time, the two bars and dining room are replete with exposed timbers, brickwork, open fireplaces etc, plus a collection of china and Worthington 'E' jugs. Regulars travel a good distance for the home cooking, but for something a little 'different' look out for theme evenings every two months, featuring menus from around the world. Private parties up to 40 are always welcome, as are children, who have a play area. Barbecue on the patio. Large car park.

THE DICKIN ARMS

Loppington.   Tel. (0939) 233471

Location:	Village centre, off Ellesmere to Shrewsbury Road.
Credit cards:	Not accepted.
Bitters:	Theakstons, Bass.
Lagers:	Becks, McEwans.

Examples of bar meals (lunch & evening, 7 days. Some dishes available lunchtime only): *homemade steak & kidney pie, cottage pie, quiche, steaks, Dickin special mixed grill, half roast duckling & orange sauce, chicken chasseur, salmon steak with hollandaise sauce, trout, scampi, omelettes, vegetarian moussaka/lasagne, mushroom nut balls in cheese sauce, jacket potatoes, salads, ploughman's, sandwiches. Kid's corner. Homemade apple pie, Alabama chocolate fudge cake, banana split. Trad. Sun. roasts.*

An old bull-baiting ring – one of only two of its kind in the country – is to be found at the front of this 17th century inn, originally owned by the Dickin family. Happily, today we prefer to take our pleasures in the more innocuous pursuits of good food and drink in convivial surrounds, such as you will find in traditional country inns like this. One visitor from the past seems to approve, for he returns in the late evening, twice a year, it is said. He finds little has changed: old timbers, brick inglenook, leaded glass and some fascinating brasses lend character. Landlord for the last five years or so has been former farmer Ed Griffiths. He welcomes children and has a play area in the garden, where occasional barbecues are held. Darts and dominoes in Public bar. Large car park.

The Squirrel Inn & Restaurant, Wollerton.

THE SQUIRREL INN & RESTAURANT

Wollerton, nr Market Drayton.   Tel. (063 084) 431
                Location: ³/4 mile from Hodnet on A53.
          Credit cards: Visa, Mastercard, Eurocard.
                Bitters: Ansells, Tetleys, Bass, Burton.
                Lagers: Lowenbrau, Skol, Castlemaine.

Examples of bar meals (all day, 7 days): *homemade lasagne, curry, gammon steak with apple & cheese, steaks, homemade burgers, whole trout with garlic butter & almonds, scampi, plaice, vegetable stroganoff, jacket potatoes, salads, ploughman's, sandwiches. Children's menu.*
Examples of restaurant meals (lunch & evening, 7 days): *roulade of smoked salmon & prawns, steaks, pigman's grill, squirrel special grill, half roast duckling in orange & brandy sauce, cutlets of pork in cider & apricot sauce, sauteed lambs kidneys (with red peppers, French beans & madeira cream sauce), whole lemon sole, salmon (in mushroom, herb & white wine cream sauce), vegetable curry, broccoli & stilton quiche. Trad. Sun. roasts.*

Charles Darwin and Clive of India are two illustrious names who have broken bread at this fine early 18th century inn. They probably also quaffed the home brewed beer (a secret cellar has been discovered) and consumed home cured meats, poultry or fish, as witnessed by the salt ovens still sited on either side of the stone fireplace. However, we lesser mortals have a wider choice of homecooked food, augmented by special evenings like Mexican, Italian or Mother's Day, courtesy of Mike Davies, landlord for two years or so. His split-level bars are full of character, with collections of pewter, shotguns and old farm implements. Children are welcome, and the garden has a play area and barbecue. Incidentally, should your pint of Skol be flat, blame Mrs Collison, who hanged herself here in 1867 and apparently likes to turn off the gas!

THE NEW INN

Shrewsbury Road, Hadnall.   Tel. (0939) 210249

Location:	Village centre, on A49.
Credit cards:	Not accepted.
Bitters:	Bass, Worthington, Highgate Mile.
Lagers:	Carling, Tennents.

Examples of bar meals (lunchtimes Mon – Sat): *gammon, various pies, sausages, burgers, salads, plaice, scampi, ploughman's, toasties, sandwiches, rolls. Trad. Sun. roasts.*

Incredible value, doubly important in current straitened circumstances, is the key to the success of this Victorian coaching inn. One feels in a time warp: prices range from 50p for fresh cut sandwiches, £1.20 for a pie with chips and peas, up to juicy gammon at £2.75, the most expensive item on the menu! One would be hard put to find the like of it anywhere for straightforward but nourishing food. Peter Maguire is the generous provider, now in his fifth year here. His pub is rather more attractive inside than out, with timber beams, two-way fireplace and collections of brasses, horse harnesses and interesting plaques. Quoits is a game rarely seen these days, but it is still played in the Public bar, along with darts and dominoes. Children are welcome, and there is a lawned garden where barbecues are held to mark special events. Large car park. Handy for Shrewsbury and Hawkstone Park.

THE NELL GWYN

Park Street, Shifnal.   Tel. (0952) 460063

Location: On main road.
Credit cards: Access, Visa, Diners, Amex.
Bitters: 2 everchanging guests.
Lagers: 2 premiums, 1 standard, everchanging.

Examples of bar meals (lunch & evening, 7 days): *speciality burgers (eg Mexican spicy chicken, fillet of fish, venison, vegetable), deep fried mixed seafood, spicy chicken wings, toasted sandwiches, jacket potatoes, homemade pizzas.*
Examples of restaurant meals (as above): *oysters Rockefeller, crawfish tails & tasso, Mexican pancake, crab filled mushrooms, steaks, Normandy duck breast in orange or peach sauce, fajitas, enchiladas, meat balls & spare ribs, seafood Jambalaya, blackened redfish, cod Yucatan style. Trad Sun roasts.*

The pub was already well established when Nell Gwyn was consorting with King Charles II, and the latter would have been familiar with the name Boscabelle – the famous Civil War battle was fought near here. This is very much 'Roundhead and Cavalier Country', so it will come as little surprise that a ghost is said to walk upstairs. In a superb Elizabethen interior, the beautiful staircase with its carved banisters deserves special mention. Modern contrivances, such as pool and video machines, are strictly confined to the Public Bar, allowing one to digest good food and ale in the peace of the other bars or restaurant (live guitar here at weekends). Dinner parties with a theme – Mexican, Caribbean, Italian etc – are a speciality, and there is a private function room. Children welcome. Garden with barbecue. Rated by Egon Ronay and Les Routiers.

THE SWAN

St. Edward Street, Leek.   Tel. (0538) 382081

      Location: Near town centre, opp. St Edwards church, on A523.

Credit cards: Not accepted.

       Bitters: Bass, Stones, guest.

       Lagers: Carling, Tennent Extra, Warsteiner.

Examples of bar meals (lunchtime only, 7 days): *braised steak, lasagne verdi, roast chicken breast, gammon, haddock, plaice, scampi, vegetable lasagne, omelettes, jacket potatoes, French sticks, sandwiches, daily specials eg chicken chasseur, lamb curry. Spotted dick, treacle sponge, death by chocolate. Trad. Sun. roasts.*

Leek·was once a centre of the silk trade, and this was one of the town's main coaching inns. Some of the original 15th century beams are still in place, and redecoration has been carried out sensitively in period style. A display case shows some of the ancient artefacts unearthed during renovation, and of additional interest is a collection of military shields and old photos of the town. So there's no shortage of character and both bars are very comfortable (one no-smoking at lunchtime), but it's also worth noting that landlord David Ellerton is a qualified chef, and has many years experience in the trade, the last three here. He presents traditional pub fare, efficiently served, in a friendly atmopshere. Well-behaved children are welcome during meal times, and the rear yard has tables and chairs in summer. Public car park opposite. Alton Towers, Buxton and The Potteries are all an easy drive.

THE THREE HORSESHOES

Blackshaw Moor, Leek.   Tel. (053 834) 296

Location:	On A53, 2 miles north of Leek.
Credit cards:	Access, Visa, Diners, Amex.
Accommodation:	6 bedrooms, with shower, col. tv's, telephone.
Bitters:	Theakstons, McEwans Export, Youngers, 80 Shillings. Guinness
Lagers:	Becks, McEwans, LA.

Examples of bar meals (lunch & evenings, 7 days): *roasts of the day, beef in red wine, vegetarian lasagne, veg. dish of day, gammon, beef & mushroom pie, chicken casserole in wine, cold meats table, sandwiches, ploughman's. Children's menu.*
Examples of restaurant meals (lunch & evening, Mon. – Sat.): *smoked trout fillet wrapped in thin pastry case served with crab sauce, pheasant casseroled in rich port wine sauce, halibut steak in champagne sauce, three slices of fillet in individual sauces, roast duckling with orange sauce of Grand Marnier & brandy.*
Afternoon teas.

Commanding fine views over the moorlands, this large country inn is very much of a family concern, run by Bill and Jill Kirk with their sons. The bars are cosy, stone walled and with low oak beams, slate floor and open fires. Both bar and candlelit restaurant offer local produce and game, together with a selection of international dishes, home cooked and served with friendly attentitivness – the well reputed carvery is particularly worth attention. The wine list is enormous, comprising of 200 bins ranging from a 1918 Pontet Canet and Chateu Lafite to popular Rhine wines. Dinner and dancing to the small hours are a special weekend treat, and very well attended. An extensive garden includes family and play areas. Facilities for private functions and weddings.

THE WHEEL INN

Leek Road, Longsdon, Stoke on Trent.   Tel: (0538) 385012
             Location: A53 Leek to Stoke.
        Credit cards: Not accepted.
             Bitters: Burton Ale, Ansells Bitter and Mild, guest.
              Lagers: Skol, Lowenbrau, Swan Light.

Examples from bar menu (lunch & evening 7 days, except Monday evening). *homemade steak pie, cottage pie, chilli, lasagne, steaks, gammon, trout, moussaka, curries, vegetarian dishes.*
Examples from restaurant menu (Tues – Sat evenings & Sun lunch) .*steaks, lobster, venison, veal, turkey with bourbon & peaches, poussin in brown ale, duck a l'orange, swordfish, salmon in orange & vermouth.*

Rural surroundings and beautiful views form the backdrop to this rather tastefully decorated pub, built about 100 years ago. Inside, various curios and collections will also please the eye, ranging from intruiging jugs to swords and brasses. But it's for good food that The Wheel is especially noted, both in the lounge bar and upstairs restaurant, coupled with personal service from Linda and Jeff Turner. There's ample scope to amuse the family, with regular barbeques in the large beer garden, robust play equipment for the children, and an aviary shortly to be joined by a pets corner.

THE PARKS

New Road, Uttoxeter.   Tel. (0889) 567482

Location:	On A522 in western outskirts of Uttoxeter.
Credit cards:	Access, Visa, Diners, Amex.
Bitters:	Marstons, Boddingtons, Youngers Scotch.
Lagers:	Becks, McKewans, Budweiser.

Examples of bar/restaurant meals (11am – 10pm, 7 days): *mushroom pepperpot, seafood dippers, mushroom stroganoff, steak, chicken a la king, pork & pineapple sweet & sour, steak kidney & mushroom pie, farmhouse mixed grill, goujons of plaice, salads. Children's menu. Trad. Sun. roasts.*

A freehouse in the truest sense, The Parks is a family pub with the boon of serving food and drink all day. From outside it is apparent that it is mock Tudor (built around the turn of the century as a private residence), but inside is modern, spacious and luxuriously furnished in period style, having been totally refurbished in 1988. The bar and separate dining room are light and airy, with large bay windows looking out over the three acres of parkland. Children are welcome, and will assuredly head for the natural play area in the grounds (barbecues are held here). It is the management's declared aim to provide the most enjoyable eating and drinking experience in the area, at reasonable prices, and the menu certainly is exceptionally varied and interesting. A striking pub, waiting for your discovery, perhaps on a visit to nearby Alton Towers or Wedgwood Centre.

THE RED LION

Newborough, nr Burton-on-Trent.   Tel. (0283) 75259
Location: B5234, nr Hoar Cross Hall.
Credit cards: Not accepted.
Accommodation: Two doubles.
Bitters: Marstons.
Lagers: Heineken, Swan Light.

Examples of bar meals (lunch & evening, 7 days): *steaks, mixed grill game pie, steak & kidney pie, chilli, vegetable lasagne, scampi, ploughman's, salads, sandwiches. Daily blackboard specials eg jugged hare, venison, rabbit, duck, chicken pie, fresh fillet plaice. Spotted dick, bread & butter pudding, death by chocolate. Trad. Sun. lunch.*

Charles II made one of his escapes here in 1651. But it is quarry of a different kind, that is game, which is the speciality of the house, for this is huntin', shootin' and fishin' country. Well-dressing events are to be seen periodically, and this is a favourite halt for hikers. Enjoying the fruits of the chase, appetisingly prepared here at The Red Lion, is another time honoured country pursuit. The building itself is some 250 years old, comprising two bars, the smaller more traditional, the larger well furnished, oak beamed with open fire. Landlord John Temple has added a new dining room recently. Barbecues are held occasionally in the lawned beer garden. Children welcome.

THE FORESTERS ARMS AND RESTAURANT

62 Wood Lane, Yoxall.   Tel: (028 375) 258

Location: A515, Lichfield to Ashbourne
Credit cards: Visa, Access, Eurocard, Mastercard.
Bitters: Marston's Pedigree & Best.
Lagers: Stela Artois, Heineken.

Examples from bar menu lunch 7 days, evening Mon – Sat): *egg & prawn mayonnaise, homemade pate, minute sirloin steak, whole baby chicken, steak & kidney pie, grilled trout, ham & mushroom omelette, burgers, salads, sandwiches.*
Examples from restaurant menu (Mon – Sat lunch & evening, trad. Sun. lunch only).*clear beef soup garnished with savoury pancakes, papiotte of salmon, chateaubriand Bearnaise, escalope of veal cordon bleu, selection of sweets, cheeseboard.*

Generous grounds, including a beer garden and play area for children, should not divert you from perhaps the most important reason for a visit – good food. As well as the examples above, consider chicken cooked in white wine with fresh fruit and tarragon, entrecote Monet Medici, in red wine, herbs, mushroom and cream sauce – something to stimulate even the most jaded of tastebuds. The 30 seater restaurant is quite separate from the two bars, one a large lounge, the other smaller but of the same status, and there's also a 24 seater function room (ring for details). The service from Irene and Ron is always friendly, and well behaved children are very welcome. Huge car park.

THE GOLDEN CUP

Main St. Yoxall, Burton on Trent.   Tel. (0543) 472295
        Location: Yoxall Village, A515.
   Credit cards: Not accepted
         Bitters: Draught Bass, Worthington Bitter.
         Lagers: Carling Black Label, Tennents Pilsner, Extra and L.A.

Examples from menu (lunchtime 7 days, evenings Tues. – Sat.): *soup of the day, beef in Bass, lasagne, chilli, steaks, mixed grill, deep fried plaice, omelettes, sandwiches. Daily specials eg steak & kidney pie, potato pie, cheese & onion pie. Vegetarian dishes on request. Homemade Bakewell tart with cream or ice cream, passion cake, homemade apple pie. Trad. Sun. lunch.*

Few other pubs can match this one for the range of facilities. In a field to the rear is a registered caravan site (bookable through the pub), and how very convenient for the 'vanners'! The children can romp in the enclosed play area in the large gardens, while parents chance their arm at boules, perhaps. But a broad section of clientele is attracted here for the good food and beer and friendly service from Mr and Mrs Guntripp and staff. A self-contained function room upstairs, recently refurbished, is suitable for weddings etc (catering as required), and downstairs this 200-year-old pub has a traditional bar and separate lounge. Well behaved children welcome. Facilities for disabled, and no steps into pub. Large car park.

THE GLOBE TAVERN

Borough Hall, Eastgate Street, Stafford.　　　　　　　　Tel. (0785) 222834

Location:　Town centre, Borough Hall.
Credit cards:　Not accepted.
Bitters:　Banks, Worthington.
Lagers:　Carling, Carlsberg, Kronenbourg.

Examples of bar/restaurant meals (lunchtime 7 days, evenings by arrangement only – min. party 25): *roasts of the day, steak & mushroom pie, braised steak, pork chops Taunton, curries, fish dishes, vegetarian lasagne, nut roast, daily specials. Approx. 30 dishes on call order menu. Children's menu.*

At the very hub of an historic county town, this elegant Victorian building was formerly the administration centre of the Borough Council, but is now given over to far worthier purposes: a 500+ seater theatre and a pub-cum-restaurant affording high standards of hygiene and cuisine – licensee Jack Tilstone is a qualified chef of 30 years standing. Refurbishment has been carried out sympathetic to a grade II listing, and amenities are first rate. In addition to two private bars, one public bar and a theatre bar, there are two function suites and a banqueting hall. Entertainment is not restricted to the theatre; the Jazz Society convenes on Sundays, there's various live music in the cabin studio and free lunchtime concerts on occasion throughout the year. Excellent disabled facilities. Car parking facilities nearby.

YE OLDE DOG & PARTRIDGE

High Street, Tutbury, nr Burton-on-Trent.   Tel. (0283) 813030
                                                       Fax. (0283) 813178

Location:	Village centre, 1/2 mile off A50.
Credit cards:	Access, Visa, Amex.
Accommodation:	5 singles, 6 doubles, 5 twins, 1 family, all en suite, tv's, hair dryers, bar fridges, tea & coffee. Special breaks.
Bitters:	Marston's Pedigree, Bass.
Lagers:	Marstons, Tennents, Stella Artois.

Examples of bar meals (lunchtimes Mon – Sat): *homemade soup, ploughman's, sailor's lunch, sandwiches, daily specials.*
Examples of restaurant meals (lunch & evening, 7 days): *carvery (noted), lasagne, Tutbury beef steak & Owd Rodger pie, champagne salmon, whole trout stuffed with prawns & wrapped in bacon, vegetarian chilli/stroganoff, cold table incl. seafood selection. Needwood Farmhouse luxury icecreams, children's treats. Trad. Sun. roasts.*

The Wars of the Roses had just begun when this superb black and white timbered edifice was raised, and 500 years on it remains wonderfully well preserved. Still a centre of local life, it came to prominence with the cruel practice of bull-running, devised by John-of-Gaunt. His name is given to the charming conference room, with its every modern facility a striking juxtaposition between ancient and modern which extends to the rest of this remarkable establishment. Most of the individual bedrooms, some with four-posters, are in an adjacent graceful Georgian building, and reached by an ornate spiral staircase. For all this splendour, long-serving host Yvette Martindale keeps prices very affordable. Highly rated by main guides. Grand piano nightly. Children welcome.

THE OLD MILL

Windmill Street, Upper Gornal, Dudley. Tel. (0902) 887707

Location: Residential area.
Credit cards: Access, Visa.
Bitters: Holdens, Old Mill own brand.
Lagers: Carling, Tennents Extra & LA, Fosters, Budweiser. Ciders.

Examples of bar meals (lunch & evening, Mon. – Sat.): *Lancashire hotpot, steak & kidney pie, beef in beer pie, fisherman's pie, chicken & mushroom pie, vegetarian pie, vegetarian cheesey bake, lasagne, veg. lasagne, chilli, curry, pork goulash, plaice with prawn & mushroom filling, chicken Kiev, Gornal sausages, rump steak, faggots & mushy peas, gammon, cod, plaice, sandwiches/rolls, ploughman's, jacket potatoes, salads. Children's menu.*

Examples of restaurant meals (evenings Wed. – Sat. Plus trad. Sun. lunch – bookings only): *roast quail in orange & brandy, cidered kidneys, prawns in hot cheese sauce; various steaks, venison casserole, honey-glazed gammon, duckling breast in honey & lemon sauce, beef in rich sauce of wine onions & mushrooms, pork in calvados & cream sauce, mixed grill, lemon sole in cider & mushroom sauce, chargrilled trout, vegetables au gratin, ratatouille provencale.*

"A country style pub in a residential area" is probably a fair description of this traditional black-and-white beamed building, on the site of an old windmill. A scan of the comprehensive menus reveals a nice blend of the time-honoured and new, all wholesome and homecooked. Proprietor John Midwood justifiably prides himself on the quality and value of the food, and excellent condition of the beers. Obviously held in esteem by locals, the pub has two soccer teams, plus darts, dominoes and quiz nights, and occasional live entertainment. With a good mix of regulars and visitors, the atmosphere is always friendly. Children are permitted to eat with parents, and there's a beer garden and two car parks.

THE PARK GATE INN & RESTAURANT

Park Gate Road, Cannock Wood, nr Rugeley.   Tel. (0543) 682223

Location: Off B5154, 2 miles from Hednesford.
Credit cards: Access, Visa.
Bitters: Ansells, Burton, Tetley.
Lagers: Skol, Lowenbrau, Swan Light.

Examples of bar/restaurant meals (lunch & evening, 7 days): *flaked mackerel & haddock with chopped egg & tomato covered in cheese sauce, 4 potato boats with various fillings, chicken & prawn sate, steaks, butterfly spiced chicken, steak & kidney pie, chicken ham & broccoli pie, spicy Cumberland sausage, devilled tiger prawns, plaice thermidor (with lobster filling), salmon in asparagus sauce, tomato & vegetable tagliatelle, daily specials (eg game in season). Lunchtime snacks. Children's menu. Trad. Sun. roasts.*

One of the eight hill forts in the country, Castle Ring was built around 500 BC, making the inn opposite, dated around 1640, seem positively recent! Once part of the Marquis of Anglesey's estate, it was the scene of many a lordly banquet, and what is now the refurbished Timbers Restaurant (available for functions) was where tenants came to pay their master's dues. So much for the history: today, under the auspices of Kevin and Trudy Pedley, it's a lively and popular pub cum restaurant, set in good walking country and, being at the highest point in Cannock Chase, affording scenic views. The irreverent strains of jazz or country and western rattle the old timbers a little every Sunday evening, when in summer there's also a barbecue. Children always welcome, and the large garden has a play area.

THE ROYAL OAK

High Street, Church Eaton, nr Stafford.   Tel. (0785) 823078
      Location: Off A518 Stafford to Telford road (turn off at Haughton).
  Credit cards: Access, Visa.
       Bitters: James Forshaws, Burtonwood Best, guests.
       Lagers: Labatts, Castlemaine.

Examples of bar/restaurant meals (lunch & evening, 7 days): *calamari & salad, steaks, Regal mixed grill, roast chicken, halibut steak in white wine & mushroom sauce, stuffed plaice, haddock, scampi, prawn salad, homemade steak & kidney pie, vegetable stroganoff, broccoli cream cheese, macaroni cheese, vegetable moussaka, sandwiches, daily specials. Trad. Sun. roasts.*

Experienced licensees John and Caroline Stenson arrived at this Edwardian pub only late in 1991. After a comprehensive refurbishment, kitchen included, they are well prepared to deal with an ever growing clientele. Well furnished in period style, the two bars are are warmed by open coal fires, and amongst the interesting decor is an evocative collection of old photographs from the early years of the century. Darts and dominoes provide further diversion, while youngsters (who are permitted inside) have a playground and pets corner in the beer garden (summer barbecues). A balanced menu presents staple English favourites, with about six vegetarian options. Well placed for Weston Park, Stafford and the beauty spots of Shropshire. Fishing on nearby canal. Ample parking.

111

THE HAND & CLEAVER INN

Butt Lane, Ranton Green, nr Stafford.   Tel. (0785) 822367

Location: One mile from Ranton village, 2¹/₂ miles off A518.
Credit cards: Access, Visa.
Bitters: Marstons Pedigree, Boddingtons, guest.
Lagers: Carling, Tennents, Heineken.

Examples of bar/restaurant meals (lunch & evening, 7 days): *garlic prawns, pancake filled with asparagus & cheese sauce, sole poached with prawn & cheese sauce, steaks, curry, chilli, homemade pies, lasagne, chicken Kiev, half duck with orange sauce, salads, jacket potatoes, sandwiches. Children's menu. Carvery on Fri./Sat./Sun.*

Part of this handsome 17th century inn was once a cowshed! In fact, the original stalls have been adapted to provide private, well upholstered 'compartments' for diners in the 80 seater restaurant. Set amongst country lanes and rural villages, it is not hard to believe that the inn was part of a farm. Its considerable age is evident from the old timbers and open fires. In addition to the restaurant are two bars, and a private room for 30 people upstairs in what was the hayloft. Brian and Winnie Smith have run their comely freehouse for more than four years, popular amongst locals, but with doors always open to visitors. The menu is varied and comprehensive, and the carvery well reputed – look out for the occasional special evening, advertised in the local press. Children are welcome, and there are no less than six climbing frames, swings and slides in the garden, which also has seating for 100 – barbecues are held here. Parking also for 100.

THE ST. GEORGE HOTEL

Castle Street, Eccleshall. Tel. (0785) 850300

Location:	Town centre.
Credit cards:	Access, Visa, Amex.
Accommodation:	10 rooms, all en suite.
Bitters:	Ansells, Burton ,Tetley, Wadworth 6X.
Lagers:	Castlemaine, Lowenbrau, Skol, L.A.

Examples of bar meals (12 – 10pm, Mon. – Sat. 12 – 2pm, 7 – 9pm Sun.): *trout, curries, gammon, chicken stuffed with prawns & lobster, steak & kidney (or mushroom) pie, lasagne, steaks, sandwiches, carvery lunch. Children's menu. Sweet selection.*
Examples of restaurant meals (lunch & evening, Mon. – Sat., plus Sun. lunch): *Dover sole, scampi lagoon, halibut bercy, duckling a l'orange, chicken Kiev, roast guinea fowl, chicken armagnac, veal cordon bleu, fillet of pork Parisienne, steaks in sauces, vegetarian dishes, special diets.*

A privately owned family concern, the St George has all the modern facilities one might associate with a larger hotel, yet retains that personal touch. Beginning as a coaching inn in 1739, it has been in its time a drapers shop, four cottages and an undertakers (one room is still known as 'The Coffin Room'). The original oak beamed bar still stands, warmed by open fires, and where home-prepared food and coffee is served all day. For an extra special meal, Knights restaurant is a memorable venue, for private parties and functions also. The bedrooms are all individual, many with exposed beams, open fires, canopied or four-poster beds, and spa baths.

THE MAINWARING ARMS

Whitmore Road, Whitmore, nr Newcastle-u-Lyme.   Tel. (0782) 680851

          Location: 1¹/₂ miles from Newcastle on A53 to Market Drayton.
     Credit cards: Not accepted.
          Bitters: Boddingtons, Marston's Pedigree, Bass, guest.
          Lagers: Carling, Stella Artois, Heineken, Tennents Extra, LA.

THE MAINWARING ARMS, WHITMORE   Nigel Edmondson 1986

Examples of bar meals (lunchtimes only, 7 days): *pork with green peppers in satay sauce, curries, chilli, gammon, grilled chicken breast with herbs & garlic, stir-fries, plaice. Trad. Sun. roast.*

The eponymous Mainwarings have owned the pub and most of the rest of the village since the 11th century, which must make it one of the oldest family concerns anywhere! The history is told in a framed document mounted on a wall. The building which now stands was built only in 1844, relatively recent but long enough to have acquired a ghost, apparently. New landlord Simon Hastings says he has not seen it, but things do seem to 'move'. Four rooms, each with open fire and exposed timbers, have recently been redecorated, with old farming and brewing implements forming the theme. One of the few concessions to the late 20th century is the unobtrusive video trivia machine on which to test the grey matter. On a sunny day, much better is to sit on the new patio, pint in hand, and admire the lovely church. Barbecues every Sunday lunch in summer, weather permitting. Children welcome up to 8pm in allocated rooms. Rated by national good pub guide. Car parking.

VARSOVIA LODGE

Hough Hill, Brown Edge, Stoke-on-Trent.   Tel. (0782) 503346
      Location: On Brown Edge, just off B5051.
  Credit cards: Access, Visa, Diners, Amex.
      Bitters: Bass, Marstons, Newcastle Exhibition, guests.
      Lagers: Carling, Tennents, Stella Artois, Carlsberg, Swan Light.

Examples of bar meals (lunch & evening 7 days, except Mon lunch): *grilled trout with almonds, steak & kidney pie, homemade pizzas, chilli, moussaka, curries, lasagne, bobotie, scampi, shepherds pie, steak, game pie, salads, rolls. Fresh strawberries in strawberry & Grand Marnier mousse, banana rum & chocolate cream, fresh cream gateau, kiwi fruit in Cointreau & white wine syllabub.*
Restaurant meals (lunchtime Tues – Fri, evenings Tues – Sat, Sun lunch 12 – 4pm): *lunches 3 courses + coffee. Evening meals Tues. to Fri. 3 courses and 6 courses table d'hote, offering wide choice for each course. Saturday evening only 6 course menu available.*

Varsovia is Polish for Warsaw, and skis mounted on the walls lend the atmosphere of a mountain lodge, so one is aware that this 18th century inn, though very solid and traditional, has a 'continental' flavour. Carefully restored, it is on two floors, with stone arches, wood panelled ceilings, feature fireplace, and luxuriously furnished. In the upstairs restaurant one can relish high quality homemade European cuisine, and proprietors Mr and Mrs Rowley take pride in employing only fresh produce. Even though near a town centre, this is a haven of peace, having a large, restful garden with fountains and ornamental pools, and magnificent views as far as Wales (70 miles away) on a clear day. Children welcome. Ample parking.

West Midlands
Locator Map

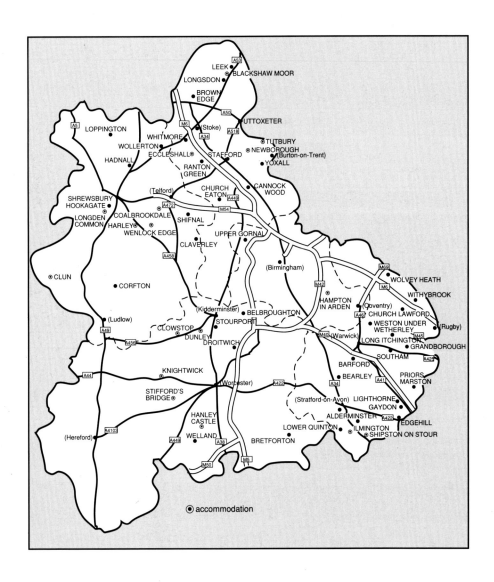

LEEK ● ● BLACKSHAW MOOR
LONGSDON ●
BROWN ● EDGE
A53
A50
A5
M6
A34 ● (Stoke)
A518 ● UTTOXETER
LOPPINGTON ●
WHITMORE ●
WOLLERTON ●
ECCLESHALL ◉
STAFFORD ◉
HADNALL ●
● TUTBURY
◉ NEWBOROUGH
(Burton-on-Trent)
● YOXALL
RANTON GREEN
(Telford)
CHURCH EATON
● CANNOCK WOOD
A472
A449
SHREWSBURY
HOOKAGATE ◉
M54
LONGDEN COMMON ●
COALBROOKDALE ◉
HARLEY ◉
WENLOCK EDGE
SHIFNAL ●
CLAVERLEY ●
UPPER GORNAL
A458
(Birmingham)
◉ CLUN
● CORFTON
M69
● WOLVEY HEATH
M6
WITHYBROOK ●
M42
HAMPTON IN ARDEN ◉
(Coventry) ◉
(Kidderminster)
● BELBROUGHTON
A46 CHURCH LAWFORD ●
(Ludlow) ●
STOURPORT ●
WESTON UNDER WETHERLEY ●
(Rugby) ●
A49
CLOWSTOP ◉
DUNLEY ◉
DROITWICH ●
M40 (Warwick)
LONG ITCHINGTON ●
M45
GRANDBOROUGH ●
A456
SOUTHAM ●
A423
KNIGHTWICK ●
BARFORD ●
A44
STIFFORD'S BRIDGE ◉
(Worcester) ●
A422
● BEARLEY
A34
PRIORS MARSTON
A41
(Stratford-on-Avon)
LIGHTHORNE ●
GAYDON
HANLEY CASTLE ●
ALDERMINSTER ●
A422
A4103
WELLAND ●
A449
A38
BRETFORTON
LOWER QUINTON ●
ILMINGTON ◉
◉ SHIPSTON ON STOUR
EDGEHILL ●
(Hereford) ●
M50
M5

◉ accommodation

East Midlands
Locator Map

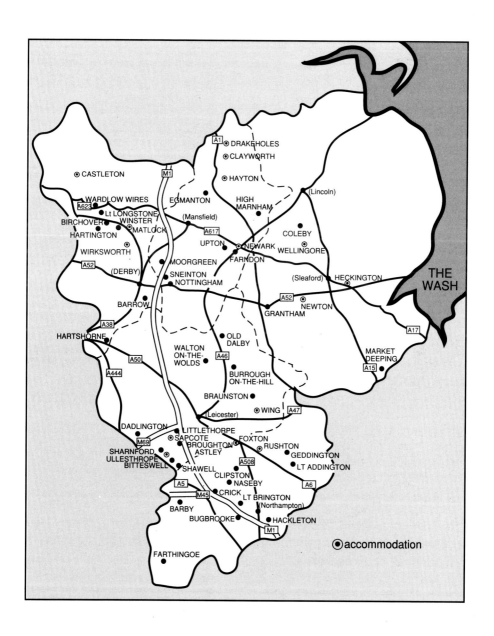

THE WASH

⊙ accommodation

INDEX

EAST MIDLANDS
Derbyshire, Nottinghamshire, Lincolnshire (west),
Leicestershire (incl. Rutland), Northamptonshire.

*accommodation

EAST MIDLANDS (continued)

WEST MIDLANDS
Warwickshire, Worcestershire, Shropshire, Staffordshire

* accommodation

* accommodation